COMING OF AGE

with the
New Republic 1938–1950

Also by Merrill D. Peterson

The Jefferson Image in the American Mind (1960)

Thomas Jefferson and the New Nation: A Biography (1970)

James Madison: A Biography in His Own Words (1974)

Adams and Jefferson: A Revolutionary Dialogue (1976)

Olive Branch and Sword: The Compromise of 1833 (1982)

The Great Triumvirate: Webster, Clay and Calhoun (1987)

Lincoln in American Memory (1994)

Edited by Merrill D. Peterson

Major Crises in American History (1962), with Leonard Levy

Democracy, Liberty and Property: State Constitutional Convention Debates of the 1820s (1966)

Thomas Jefferson: A Profile (1966)

The Portable Thomas Jefferson (1975)

Thomas Jefferson: Writings (1984)

Thomas Jefferson: A Reference Biography (1986)

The Virginia Statute for Religious Freedom: Its Evolution and Consequences in American History (1988), with Robert Vaughan

Visitors to Monticello (1989)

The Political Writings of Thomas Jefferson (1993)

COMING OF AGE

with the
New Republic 1938–1950

MERRILL D. PETERSON

University of Missouri Press

Columbia and London

Library of Congress Cataloging-in-Publication Data

Peterson, Merrill D.
    Coming of age with the New Republic, 1938–1950 /
Merrill D. Peterson.
        p.   cm.
    ISBN 0-8262-1257-3 (alk. paper)
    1. New Republic (New York, N.Y.)   2. Liberalism—
United States—History—20th century.   3. Historians—
United States Biography.   4. Peterson, Merrill D.
I. Title.
PN4900.N328P48   1999
051–dc21   99-44264
                                                          CIP

DESIGNER: ELIZABETH K. YOUNG

TYPESETTER: BOOKCOMP, INC.

PRINTER AND BINDER: THOMSON-SHORE, INC.

TYPEFACE: USHERWOOD

Acknowledgments appear on page 131.

TO NINI ALMY

Contents

COMING OF AGE

with the

New Republic 1938–1950

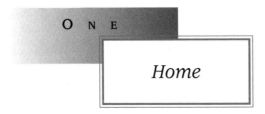

ONE

Home

I began my senior year of high school in September 1938 against the drumbeat of the German-Czech crisis in Europe. Growing up deep in the heart of the country, in Manhattan, Kansas, I had been little troubled by the shock waves of war and revolution coming from beyond America's borders. My ignorance and complacency were shattered in this crisis, however, and I quickly shed the cocoon of midwestern isolationism. Until that time, radio had been for my family a medium of entertainment, featuring the likes of Jack Benny and Charlie McCarthy. During that critical month, it became our source for dramatic international news. We huddled over the radio, listening to live reports from foreign correspondents like William L. Shirer and Edward R. Murrow and the voices of Adolf Hitler and Neville Chamberlain, all orchestrated from a New York studio by H. V. Kaltenborn, his throat filled with the sounds of disaster. Finally, in the climactic conference at Munich, Britain and France yielded to Germany's demands for the dismemberment of Czechoslovakia. The world would shortly turn the final corner and plunge into a devastating war. If this truth had not yet penetrated my consciousness, it soon would. In retrospect, certainly, I saw that the Munich *appeasement*—henceforth a dirty word in my political vocabulary—was the catalyst of my quest for intellectual maturity.

The coming of the Second World War overshadowed my senior year in Manhattan High School. I had been born in this city of about ten thousand people, where the prairie meets the plains, and though my family had moved away, then back, several times, Manhattan was the only town I called home. My father—old enough to have been my grandfather—was an ordained Baptist minister, sans pulpit, who had a hard time making a living. Mother filed for divorce when I was in the third grade. Manhattan was the seat of Kansas State Agricultural College (KSAC), a land-grant institution, and my mother supported me and my two older brothers by running a boardinghouse for college students. She calculated, quite accurately, that her sons would have a better chance of getting college degrees if we lived in a college town. Times were tough—it was the Great Depression—but both my brothers went on to graduate from KSAC and I started there. The college, together with the boardinghouse mix, provided links to the larger culture. Kansas City, 125 miles due east, was our metropolis; we read the *Kansas City Star* and, on rare occasions, went there for a Blues baseball game or a road show at the Music Hall.

Reinforcing the impact of events in Europe was a required senior-year social studies course called American Problems, taught by William R. Purkaple. He was an exotic in Manhattan. He didn't look like anyone else; he didn't think like anyone else. Where he came from I never learned. He was a loner. Once I visited him in his rented quarters across from the school, and I saw at a glance how austere his life was. He furnished his classroom, I suppose on his own nickel, with many magazines—weeklies, monthlies, quarterlies—devoted to public affairs. These ranged from "journals of opinion," *Nation, New Republic,* even *New Masses,* to the *Saturday Review of Literature, Time, Current Events, Harper's,* and *Atlantic Monthly,* and more specialized monthlies like *Survey Graphic.* Through the magazines and his inspired teaching, Mr. Purkaple parted the curtain for his students on the exciting world of ideas, politics, and culture that, until then, had lain beyond our ken.

I became a serious reader. I used my meager earnings as a nighttime soda jerk at the Varsity Drug Store to join the Book-of-the-Month Club (BOMC). A time came when this seemed to be a matter for apology in my life. But, of course, the BOMC performed a valuable service in the vast stretches of the country where there were few, if any, outlets for current books and no literary guidance to speak of. As I remember, the first book received—it must have been a membership gift—was T. E. Lawrence's *Seven Pillars of Wisdom,* which proved too deep for me at seventeen. But other BOMC selections, like *An American Doctor's Odyssey* by Victor Heiser, who had circled the globe as a public health physician, and Ignazio Silone's anti-fascist *Bread and Wine,* linger in my memory after sixty years.

The mention of Silone suggests the leftward drift of my political opinions. Purkaple's influence was all in that direction. As late as the 1936 presidential election, my sympathies followed the rooted Republicanism of my parents and the overwhelming majority of Kansans. The Republican candidate in that election was Alfred M. Landon, our esteemed governor, and I was proud to wear the sunflower button with the slogan, "Off the Rocks with Landon and Knox." But President Roosevelt's land-slide victory gave me pause, and then his courageous fight against the obstructionism of the Supreme Court earned my admiration and support ever after. That fight proved to be the exquisite case in American political annals of losing the battle but winning the war. Certain of my mother's boarders nudged me toward Democratic allegiance. Some of these were sons and daughters of farm families succored by New Deal agricultural pro-grams. Others, curiously, were Jews from New York City who came to KSAC to study veterinary medicine. Quotas barred them from admission to Cornell and other east-ern schools. My acquaintance with Jews, Jewishness, and anti-Semitism began with the transients in my mom's boardinghouse, and the rapport I felt then stayed with me always. (Later I guessed that Mr. Purkaple might have been Jewish, but I never knew.) As editor of the school newspaper in my senior year, I wrote a column, "As I See It," where I occasionally aired heterodox political opinions. In one of our weekly assemblies, I recited a defiant proletarian speech from Clifford Odets's *Waiting for Lefty.* I had the platform because of my extracurricular activity in drama and debate. The latter, in particular, built self-confidence and added to my acquaintance with national issues and events.

Of the magazines I had read in Purkaple's class, my favorite was the *New Republic*. I began to subscribe to it. It became my guide and preceptor for the next ten years. At the time I knew nothing of the magazine's history; that knowledge came later. Herbert Croly, the founding editor in 1914, had some years earlier written a landmark book of progressive reform ideology, *The Promise of American Life*. "It became a reservoir for all political writing," as Felix Frankfurter observed. A double perversion had entered the American dream at the outset, Croly argued. The democratic ideal was associated with fears of central authority and responsibility, while the national ideal was compromised by fears of democracy. To overcome this division, Croly said, democracy must become a force for national organization and achievement rather than timidity and drift. Similarly, in foreign affairs the United States must break the shell of isolationism and assume a positive and responsible place among the nations. The *New Republic* was dedicated to these high purposes.

In 1939 the journal published a twenty-fifth–anniversary supplement entitled "The Promise of American Life," and I got a glimpse of its history as well as of the range of its coverage of American politics and culture. The lead article by George Soule, an associate editor, "Toward a Planned Society," showed the magazine's collectivist bent. John Chamberlain, a contributor, addressed "Croly and the American Future." Malcolm Cowley, the literary editor, wrote "A Farewell to the 1930s." And Archibald MacLeish supplied a verse-manifesto, "America Was Promises," with the shrill refrain, "The promises are theirs who take them." There were articles on the promise in education, in organized labor, and on the farm. Bruce Bliven, the editor, a staunch liberal who had made his career in journalism, contributed "Notes on the American Character." The *New Republic* was often coupled with its friendly rival, the *Nation,* which had a much longer history. Both magazines were published in New York. Both were left-liberal, though the *Nation,* under Freda Kirchwey, was a shade further left. It lacked, moreover, the backing of a wealthy publisher. The *New Republic* had been established by Willard Straight and his wife, Dorothy Whitney, both well off financially; and Whitney continued to subsidize the journal after Straight's death and her marriage to an Englishman, Leonard Elmhirst. Neither magazine sought advertisements; neither had a circulation above 40,000. Both counted on a loyal readership.

When I became a subscriber, the *New Republic* was beginning to focus on President Roosevelt's candidacy and reelection to a precedent-shattering third term. While the president kept silent, speculation centered on a number of potential successors, none of them satisfactory, who waited in the wings. No creditable Republican challenger emerged until Wendell Willkie burst upon the scene in the election year. The great reforms of the New Deal were not likely to be overturned in any event. In July 1939, Harold Laski, the leading British student of American affairs, contributed a two-part article, "America Revisited," which offered a highly favorable report on the nation's progress over the past decade. The problem of a mature capitalist economy persisted, he wrote, but the political mind of the country had risen to a higher level. The epoch of laissez faire was over, and the country had acquired "a sense of the State," with its benefits, for the first time. The profoundly isolationist temper of the people disturbed Laski; nevertheless, he wrote, "The feeling about America that one has on returning to Europe is of immense energy and exhilaration."

The prospect of European war clouded every political endeavor. The New Deal had been built on a fragile intersectional alliance of eastern and western Democrats, with scattered southern support. Increased administration attention to the totalitarian threat abroad alienated midwestern isolationists in particular. They struck back, attempting to keep America from becoming involved in a war. One such attempt was the Ludlow Amendment. Named for an Indiana congressman, it would have required a national referendum on a declaration of war except in the event of an invasion of the United States. Defeated when it came to a vote in Congress in 1938, it was revived the following year by "Young Bob" La Follette of Wisconsin. The president voiced his opposition in a letter to the Speaker of the House: "Such an amendment to the Constitution . . . would cripple the President in his conduct of foreign relations, and it would encourage other nations to believe they could violate American rights with impunity." Again, the amendment was narrowly defeated. The *New Republic* breathed a sigh of relief. But the "guns over butter" choices evident in Roosevelt's annual budgets gave the editors concern. Increases of two-thirds in military appropriations were accompanied by slashes in the Works Progress Administration (WPA) and other relief programs, despite continued high unemployment.

For the first time since 1933, the president proposed no new reform legislation to Congress. The *New Republic* referred scathingly to "business appeasement." Heywood Broun, a contributor, entered a hopeless plea to "Save the Arts Projects," maintaining their importance on the cultural front against fascism. Hallie Flanagan, head of WPA's Federal Theater, which was abandoned, later appealed in vain to restore it and the 7,900 jobs that were lost. While mounting rearguard defenses on this front, the editors rallied to Roosevelt's initiatives in foreign affairs, beginning with the repeal of the arms embargo of the Neutrality Act and the adoption of the "cash-and-carry" rule meant to benefit Britain and France. (The provision authorized export of arms and munitions to belligerents for cash and transit in their own vessels.) This was accomplished after the war began.

In the run-up to the election, the magazine published a special section, "The New Deal in Review, 1936–40," and concluded: "The New Deal, even in its second term, has clearly done far more for the general welfare of the country and its citizens than any administration in the previous history of the nation." Sometimes liberalism's cultural and political fronts came together in compelling fashion. The Farm Security Administration (FSA), created in 1937 to improve the lot of the nation's rural poor, has been called "the social conscience of the Second New Deal." A year and a half later, John Steinbeck's *The Grapes of Wrath,* the anguished story of dust-bowl refugees in sunny California, appeared to critical acclaim. Reviewing it in the *New Republic,* Cowley, although he did not think the novel equal to the best works of Ernest Hemingway and John Dos Passos, nevertheless placed it in the same company, and he linked its message to the long poem "Land of the Free" by Archibald MacLeish. John Ford's motion picture, based on Steinbeck's novel, came out the following year. Otis Ferguson, the magazine's frequently caustic film critic, called it "the most mature motion picture that has ever been made, in feeling, in purpose, and in the use of the medium." At the same time Carey McWilliams's brilliant study of migrant labor, *Factories in the Field,* was published. McWilliams was California state commissioner of immigration and housing and an occasional contributor to the *New Republic.* The magazine followed the congressional hearings on migratory farm labor then going forward under Senator La Follette's chairmanship, calling them "the most careful and complete job of book reviewing that has ever been done." Not to be forgotten were the heartrending photographs that Dorothea Lange made for the FSA. Living on the border of the dust bowl, I knew something about its human costs and was fascinated by all this.

For twenty years the *New Republic* had agonized over the failure of Wilsonian idealism—so much of its own making—in the Great War. It would not be startled into this new one, however great the provocation. Just after the war broke out in Europe, an editorial appeared titled "1914 Repeats Itself." The accuracy of its prediction was underscored by the sinking of the *Athenia* with three hundred American refugees on board. In June the editors had solicited responses from friends and contributors on "America and the Next War." Seven policy options, ranging from strict neutrality to alliance with Britain and

France, were offered. Most respondents favored the former, perhaps with some leaning toward benevolent neutrality. This coincided, generally, with the verdict of a *Fortune* poll taken in August: 65.6 percent of those polled said that if the Western democracies went to war with the "dictator states," the United States should not intervene. The *New Republic* agreed with Roosevelt on "cash-and-carry" neutrality and hoped this might tip the balance in favor of the West in Europe. Fears that the European war would jeopardize reform at home were exaggerated, according to George Soule, reporting from Washington in late September: "A month ago the New Deal was retreating. The question was whether it would survive the next election, in view of the drift to the Right." Now, said Soule, the chances of Roosevelt running for a third term and winning were "enormously increased," and the national defense effort promised to create jobs and expand and strengthen economic planning and control at the federal level. In sum, the war might save the New Deal. In this judgment Soule, surprisingly, found himself in agreement with sour-headed John T. Flynn, the magazine's financial columnist, who was as conservative as Soule and Bliven were liberal. "America has a new sweetheart. She is *La Guerre,*" Flynn wrote, detecting in defense preparations a left-wing conspiracy.

The fact that the war began in the immediate aftermath of the Nazi-Soviet Non-Aggression Pact changed its complexion for many *New Republic* readers and threw them off balance politically. I was too young at the time to understand the shock of this event to the Left, but upon revisiting the columns some sixty years later, I found the force of it perfectly evident. The Popular Front, as it was called, had taken form internationally during the Spanish Civil War. (Its best expression in domestic politics was the government of Léon Blum in France.) The war drew to a tragic close, and the victorious Fascists under Gen. Francisco Franco came to power in Madrid not long after I subscribed to the *New Republic*. Appeasement took the form of nonintervention in Spain. The United States, Great Britain, and France refused arms to the Loyalists, the defenders of the Republic, under a specious neutrality, for the Fascists were openly aided and supplied by Germany and Italy. The Soviet Union supported the Loyalists, and the Communists took the lead in organizing international brigades to fight in Spain. Thus several thousand American volunteers were organized in the Lincoln Battalion.

The war in Spain was a far-off, shadowy event in my mind. But I read André Malraux's *Man's Hope,* which captured the heroism and tragedy of the Loyalist cause. The same vibrations came through Vincent Sheean's report *Not Peace but a Sword* in 1939. Sheean was a sort of Byronic foreign correspondent whose reporting on war and revolution from Shanghai to Madrid, beginning with *Personal History* in 1935, became part of the literary consciousness of a generation of Americans. Thinly veiled romance combined with the Marxist dialectics of "the long view" were the author's stock-in-trade. Sheean's account of "The Last Volunteer," Jim Lardner, son of Ring Lardner and the last American killed in Spain, was heartrending. On the Left a halo of idealism surrounded this lost cause. Whose pulse did not beat faster upon hearing the words of La Pasionaria, the indefatigable Spanish Bolshevik? "It is better to die on your feet than live on your knees." Spain was the only place in Europe where the march of Fascism was resisted; when, after two and a half years, gallant Madrid surrendered, appeasement won its last victory.

Disillusion, however, was already setting in. John Dos Passos, having completed his great trilogy of novels, *U.S.A.,* decided to go to Spain to report about it and to satisfy his own curiosity. He also planned to look up his friend José Robles, a teacher at Johns Hopkins University, who had been vacationing in his homeland with his family when war broke out. Robles had remained to fight in defense of the Republic but, alarmingly, had not been heard from for some time. After a long search, Dos Passos discovered that Robles had been shot by the Communists as a fascist spy. Others who had gone to Spain at the same time, among them Ernest Hemingway, said Spanish Loyalists had killed Robles as a traitor. Dos Passos was incredulous. Hemingway concluded he was "naive," perhaps a "Trotskyist." After he returned from Spain, Dos Passos turned the story of Robles into the story of Glenn Spotswood, the protagonist of the novel *Adventures of a Young Man.* Spotswood, a rebel-idealist, enlists in the International Brigade and is betrayed and killed by the Communists. Dos Passos had for years traveled on the margins of the American Communist Party. He exemplified the Popular Front. The 1939 novel marked his farewell to all that. Malcolm Cowley, reviewing it in the *New Republic,* called the work disappointing and went on to say that the plot was based upon an outright political fabrication. Dos Passos responded, maintaining the basic truth of his account, from which it followed that the Popular Front was not only dead but unconscionable. A year and some months later Cowley gave a rave review to Hemingway's *For Whom the Bell Tolls*. It was written in the spirit of the International Brigade, and although it showed gradual disillusionment, said Cowley, it was true to the noble spirit of the cause for which the hero, Robert Jordan, died.

What finally doomed the Popular Front's strategy was, of course, the Nazi-Soviet Pact. Louis Fischer, the *Nation's* roving correspondent, who had spent many years in Moscow, then fought in Spain, asked himself why he had not denounced Joseph Stalin and his repressive regime in 1937 at the time of the infamous "purge" trials; and he answered, "It is not easy to throw away the vision to which you have been attached for fifteen years." Besides, he said, in foreign affairs Russia offered the only hope of stopping Hitler. Now that calculation was upset by the Non-Aggression Pact. It was, said Fischer, "totally inde-fensible" inasmuch as Moscow knew Britain and France had begun to turn away from appeasement. Malraux, writing to him from Paris, declared laconically, "We are back to zero." Granville Hicks, the American Communist and literary editor of the *New Masses,* who had swallowed the travesty of the Moscow Trials, was dumbfounded: "Jesus Christ, that knocks the bottom out of everything." Hicks immediately resigned from the party. Explaining his action in an open letter to the *New Republic,* Hicks said it was inspired less by the pact itself than by the party's fumbling response to it. The party was utterly unprepared for the Soviet demarche and issued an apologetic devoid of reason, acknowledging, said Hicks, "that if the leaders could not defend the Soviet Union intelligently, they would defend it stupidly." Sheean, who had helped to aid thousands of Spanish refugees, contributed to the magazine a thoughtful two-part article, "*Brumaire: The Soviet Union as a Fascist State.*" The Communist Revolution, in other words, had entered its Napoleonic phase. This was reflected in the Soviet handling of foreign affairs: cautious, defensive policy became aggressive and imperial. The Soviet state, said Sheean, had gone from parody of fascism to partner of fascism. The editors, in response, thought Sheean went too far and did not fairly weigh the USSR's realistic fears of Nazi Germany abetted by the Western appeasers.

That those fears were, indeed, realistic was the burden of Frederick L. Schuman's astute analysis in *Night Over Europe,* the third and final volume of his great series charting the diplomacy leading to World War II. Schuman, an academic scholar, was an occasional contributor to the *New Republic,* and I later encountered his brilliant book *The Nazi Dictatorship* in college. Winston Churchill, in 1939, would declare Soviet foreign policy "a riddle wrapped in a mystery inside an enigma." But it was neither riddle nor mystery nor enigma to Schuman. In his second volume, *Europe on the Eve,* he had advanced the bold hypothesis that the calculus of the Western appeasers was to surrender Central Europe to Hitler in order to foment war between Nazi Germany and the Soviet Union. Stalin saw this. At first he approached Britain and France for guarantees of his western borders, and when he did not get them, he turned to Hitler, who agreed to pay the price in exchange for Soviet nonbelligerency in the war on the "imperialist" powers. Many objected to the thesis when Schuman advanced it, but the course of diplomacy had only confirmed it, he argued, and so he reiterated it. I, too, was skeptical of Schuman's thesis. It was realpolitik run amok and terribly discreditable to the Western powers. Schuman's *New Republic* article "Machiavelli in Moscow," which appeared some time later, drew a rebuttal from the editors. One thing was clear: As long as the Nazi-Soviet Pact held, the only way the West could win the war was with the full support of the United States.

T w o

World War

I had just begun my freshman year in college when the war began. The campus, where the neighborhood gang had cavorted in my youth, was only a block and a half away from the boarding house. At one corner it emptied into Aggieville, the college business district, and there the Varsity Drug Store, my employer, was located. I entered college as a premed student. My early ambition was warmly supported by my mother and my boss, "Dad" Armstrong, and my first-year program reflected that. However, I soon questioned whether my talents ran to medicine. Increasingly, I was drawn toward politics and international affairs.

That fall was the period of the "Phony War." The *New Republic* published an amazing poem, "September 1, 1939," by a new arrival on our shores, W. H. Auden. The poet sits in a dive on Fifty-second Street, New York, "Uncertain and afraid / As the clever hopes expire / Of a low dishonest decade."

> Faces along the bar
> Cling to their average day:

The light must never go out,
The music must always play,
All the conventions conspire
To make this fort assume
The furniture of home;
Lest we should see where we are,
Lost in the haunted wood,
Children afraid of the night
Who have never been happy or good.

At about the same time, the poet's compatriot H. N. Brailsford filed one of his periodic reports from London. His articles were among the best contributions to the magazine during the war. Surprisingly, Brailsford wrote, morale was high. The people were stout of heart. "Britain has many blunders to regret but it has set its course. It will risk everything to preserve the moral values of Western civilization. The stake is nothing other and nothing less." In the East, Russia appropriated the Polish borderlands, gobbled up the Baltic countries, and invaded Finland. All this was an aftershock of the Nazi-Soviet Pact, indeed the predictable consequence of it. The *New Republic* denounced the invasion as "unprovoked aggression." Even Schuman agreed with the assessment. The Russian invasion was worse than a crime, it was a great blunder. Sympathy for little Finland—the only country to have paid its World War I debts—swept the United States.

Bruce Bliven, "a pacifist at heart," as he confessed in his autobiography, was determined not to repeat the country's, and the magazine's, mistake of the First World War. Max Lerner, who had drifted from the *Nation* to the *New Republic,* observed in 1940, "Every generation of thinkers tends to act negatively in terms of its experience in some analogous situation within its memory." And so the *New Republic,* which bore the brunt of Randolph Bourne's censure for riding Wilsonian ideals into Europe's war in 1917, sought "to find atonement for its sins in the First World War by isolationism in the present one." Except for the "cash-and-carry" amendment of the Neutrality Act, the magazine opposed every move and gesture toward intervention. One reason for this was fear of a backlash at home. Popular sentiment was isolationist. The Communist Party had not disappeared. Many fellow travelers had recanted, and the party could now be tarred with the same brush as the Nazis, but its membership still hovered around 100,000. The hunt for Reds, spurred on by Martin Dies and the House Un-American Activities Committee and assisted by the FBI, as well as by grassroots vigilantes, was stepped up. Bliven and Soule conceded that the mask had been ripped off twenty years' blind obsession with the Soviet Union, yet they feared the consequences of equally blind revulsion. When the American Civil Liberties Union voted to bar Communists and Fascists and their sympathizers from office in the organization, and expelled Elizabeth Gurley Flynn, a known Communist, the editors took a deep breath and concurred in the decision.

The war in the West began with the German invasion of Denmark and Norway in April. The stunning German conquest showed the inconsequence of British seapower before the enemy's airpower. "Let Britain lose the Norway campaign and the empire of the mistress of the seas will be eroded like a sandbank in a flooded torrent," the magazine's editors wrote, but the campaign was already lost when this was published. The time had come to face the real possibility of Hitler's winning the war. "This nation has to be ready for allied disaster in Europe." The United States had to look to its defenses, reelect Roosevelt, and strengthen democracy at home, lest it fall victim to the decay that afflicted the tired capitalist democracies of Europe. The *New Republic*'s noninterventionist stance was unchanged.

Already, I was becoming critical of that view. In the general run of reading, I encountered Lewis Mumford's *Men Must Act,* a tract for the times that took aim at the *New Republic*'s position. Mumford, an independent radical and cultural critic, had been attempting to rouse the country to the dangers of totalitarianism, both Left and Right, since 1938, when he wrote "a call to arms" in the *New Republic,* which listed him as a contributing editor. While it failed to shake the complacency that prevailed in the front office, the response from readers was sufficient to divert the author from his philosophical projects. The outlook for humanity was bleaker than it had been at any time since the Black Death, Mumford declared. Barbarism had returned. And how had this been allowed to happen? "Out of the spinelessness of 'liberalism' the backbone of fascism has been created." Liberalism, of course, was what the *New Republic* professed. A morally aroused, armed United States could alone save humanity, Mumford preached.

At the end of April, the *New Republic* carried a six-page article—twice the usual length—"The Corruption of Liberalism" from Mumford's pen. "The record of liberalism in the last decade is one of shameful evasion and inept retreat," he wrote. Even today, when the barbarians are at the gate, liberals remain passive and confused. Mumford discussed the two historic elements of liberalism: The humanist, as exemplified by Jefferson and Mill, and the pragmatic, which was the product of industrialism and the machine. The latter repressed the world of values, feeling, and imagination. It denied evil, except only as the absence of good. It suffered from "emotional anesthesia." A snake in one's path is an object of study and debate for the liberal, not an object to arouse fear and the resolution to scotch it. "To be too virtuous to live is one of the characteristic moral perversions of liberalism in our generation." This was strong stuff. Mumford continued and developed the constructive part of his argument in *Faith for Living* (1940). Pleading for a return to communal life almost religious in nature, he proposed universal service by the young, curtailment of civil liberties to ensure survival, and similar measures that outraged many liberals. Mumford's philippic has sometimes been compared to Randolph Bourne's "War and the Intellectuals," addressed to the editors of the *New Republic* in 1917. But Bourne's complaint against the "pragmatism" of John Dewey, Croly, Walter Lippmann, and the others was that it led them to intervene in an unjust cause, while Mumford's complaint was on grounds of inaction in a just one.

The editors filed their dissent immediately. Most liberals would not recognize themselves in Mumford's characterization, they said. Sadly, he seemed to be making the same mistake as the Nazis, embracing an obscurantist and destructive mysticism, and flailing wildly at all nonbelievers. Cowley, when he reviewed *Faith for Living,* thought Mumford abandoned democracy in order to save it. "Behind the patriotic vision is the barbed wire of concentration camps." Yet for all his rhetoric, Mumford did not call for a declaration of war. His real target seemed to be the same as the *New Republic*'s: isolationism. "It is not a mark of barren isolationism," the editors concluded, "to believe with all one's heart and soul that the best contribution Americans can make to the future of humanity is to fulfill democracy in the United States."

That tired excuse for weakness and timidity in addressing the war abroad repelled me when I first read it, and it is just as irksome now. Despite the somewhat hysterical tone of "The Corruption of Liberalism," I felt basic agreement with it and was glad to see Mumford's militant plea in the pages of the *New Republic*. I said this in a letter to the editors and took pleasure in its publication several weeks later. (This was the first time anything with my name attached had appeared in print.) The article brought a flood of letters pro and con. The responses ran three to one against Mumford, according to the editors. I described myself as a college student who had no wish to die on the battlefields of Europe or Asia, but, I continued, like Lewis Mumford, "I have the courage to believe in the principles of democracy, and the realization of the unalterable fact that those very principles—of freedom, justice, the supremacy of the individual over the state— are at stake in Europe today." Regrettably, I concluded, my admiration for the *New Republic* had slipped of late "because of the editors' inane stupidity in refusing to recognize the necessity of American intervention in the war." This last was sophomoric at best and, in retrospect, unfair, yet my mind and heart were in the right place. And after all, I was a sophomore. Five weeks after his article appeared, Mumford resigned as a contributing editor of the journal. Waldo Frank, Mumford's friend and fellow contributor, whose prose I could never penetrate, resigned as well.

The next six or seven weeks saw the Nazi blitzkrieg on the western front and the fall of France. The editors, like Churchill, had subscribed to the theory of the superiority of the French army. There was nothing left of that theory. Americans began to talk seriously of "hemispheric solidarity" against fascism. Building on Roosevelt's Good Neighbor Policy, it found favor in the State Department. It was the current, indeed, it seemed to me, the recurrent intercollegiate debate topic, and I have never known as much about Latin America as I knew then. George Soule, foreseeing German conquest of the continent, said it was too late to defeat fascism in Europe. Defense would have to be concentrated on the Atlantic frontier and in a gallant Britain. This underscored the urgency of conversion and mobilization of American industry for war production. The magazine published a supplement treating the subject. It concluded with Lerner's article "America in a Totalitarian World." In his book of 1938, *It is Later than You Think,* which I admired, he had called for comprehensive economic planning to meet the looming crisis. Unfortunately, the call had not been heeded; now he renewed it. The war for Lerner and liberals like him would become a vehicle for the realization of "democratic collectivism" as well as for its primary purpose, the defeat of totalitarianism.

In June, not long after Mumford's blast, the *New Republic* published an address by Archibald MacLeish, poet and Librarian of Congress, "Post-war Writers and Pre-War Readers," which had been delivered before the Association for Adult Education in New York City. To me it read like a counterpoint to Mumford's plea. This address closely followed one read before the American Philosophical Society, "The Irresponsibles," which the *Nation* had published. There MacLeish raised the question: Why did the writers and scholars of our generation fail to oppose the forces of destruction in Europe? His answer was that they had insulated themselves from the real world and evaded the responsibility of moral choice. "Where the modern scholar escapes from the moral judgments of the mind by taking the disinterested man of science as his model, the modern writer escapes by imitation of the artist." The second address was the more damning, and it caused a furor. In my memory it melded into the first and took its title. MacLeish's point of departure was an article published by John Chamberlain five or six months earlier, "American Youth Says Keep Out," based upon a touring survey of student opinion. "Everywhere the isolationist strain ran deep," the author wrote, and students dismissed appeals to patriotism and moral responsibility as propaganda. MacLeish wrote, "If the younger generation in America is distrustful of all words, distrustful of all moral judgments for better or worse, then it is incapable of using the only weapon with which fascism can be fought—the moral conviction that fascism is evil and that a free society of free men is worth fighting for." He went on to lay the responsibility for the corruption of the "pre-war readers" upon the "post-war writers," himself included, of the generation Gertrude Stein had called lost. The novels of Dos Passos, Hemingway, Ford, Remarque, and others were filled with contempt for all statements of principle and belief. In *Three Soldiers,* Dos Passos said civilization was "nothing but a vast edifice of sham," and Hemingway wrote in *Farewell to Arms,* "I was always embarrassed by the words sacred, glorious, and sacrifice, and the expression in vain. . . . Abstract words such as glory, honor, courage, or hallow were obscene beside the concrete names of villages, the numbers of roads, the names of rivers, the numbers of regiments and the dates." The bitter fruits of the Great War had left the younger generation defenseless against a ruthless enemy. In the mouth of a man well known for saying

> A poem should not mean
> But be

the indictment came with some ill grace, but MacLeish, in becoming a "public poet," had embraced a different muse. The fall of France had cut him to the bone and turned him into a man of action. The editors, responding to MacLeish, said he was right about the generation gap. In the universities, the professors, having apparently shaken off the postwar writers, were ready for war while the students were opposed or apathetic. But MacLeish was wrong to blame the writers for this condition. Edmund Wilson, who never approved of MacLeish, charged that he confused the disillusionment of the postwar writers with abandonment of principle. Hemingway

defended himself in a letter to his old friend. He had
fought fascism every way he knew how and suffered
no remorse for anything he had written. He warned
MacLeish against jingoism and suggested he wanted "a
fascism to end fascism."

At about this time, summer 1940, Frank Rickel, a fellow Manhattanite and sometime debate partner, and I un-
dertook to form a militant youth organization. Forensics,
my preferred intercollegiate sport, lay in the background
of influences playing upon me. Not only did it add significantly to my acquaintance with public issues and teach
me the importance of argument and decision upon them,
but it also expanded my horizons geographically and
figuratively. Speech and debate took me outside Kansas
for the first time in my life. I attended debate tournaments
in Iowa and Colorado. I won the Missouri Valley Orator-
ical Contest at the University of Arkansas and pocketed
the twenty-five–dollar prize, the most money I had ever
received at one time. And in my sophomore year the
debate coach, Norm Webster, took three of us in his car on
a tour that encompassed New Orleans, Miami, New York,
Pittsburgh, and then home. We debated at campuses all
along the route.

Rickel and I were influenced, too, by the national
Committee to Defend America by Aiding the Allies, nom-
inally led by William Allen White, the famous Kansas
newspaperman. After Italy declared war on Britain in
June, President Roosevelt delivered his most combative
speech to date, denouncing Mussolini's "stab in the back"
and pledging all aid, short of war, to Britain. The *New
Republic* said the speech marked a change of policy from

neutrality to "partisan non-belligerency." Brailsford, describing himself as "your oldest contributor"—his association went back to 1915—sent "An Appeal from England." Voicing his confidence in Prime Minister Churchill, he argued against America's "fortress mentality," saying it only prolonged the world's agony, and pleaded for immediate entrance into the war. The editors stuck to their opinion. Conceding they had underestimated Germany's power, they continued to say the United States could do more for democracy by remaining at peace. Three months later Brailsford renewed the plea with the same result. Behind his thinking was the bold idea set forth by Clarence Streit in his book *Union Now*, published in 1939. The author had been the Geneva correspondent of the *New York Times*. That post had given him a vantage point on the failure of collective security. I was intrigued by Streit's leading analogy from American history: the League of Nations failure, like the original league of states, the Articles of Confederation, might be overcome by a federal union of all the people as in the United States Constitution. Streit proposed to begin the new union with fifteen founder democracies: the United States, Britain and the Commonwealth nations, and those of Western Europe. This excluded Asia, Latin America, Africa (except for white-ruled South Africa), and the USSR. That selectivity was a serious fault, as was Streit's failure to face the economic disparities and discord among the nations. By 1941, when most of the democracies had disappeared, Streit altered the plan and the book's title to *Union Now with Britain*. Such a proposal, of course, assumed an American declaration of war.

Democracy's Volunteers, as we named our student association, stopped short of calling for a declaration of war but advocated "All possible aid from the nations of the Western Hemisphere to Great Britain and China," together with "non-intercourse" with Germany, Italy, Japan, and nations under their control. Neither Rickel nor I had participated in a national student organization. It was our impression, however, that they tended to be dominated by well-organized Communist minorities and were isolationist or pacifist in outlook. This could be gleaned from Irwin Ross's periodic reports in the *New Republic*. The American Youth Congress (AYC), the umbrella organization, held a Citizenship Institute in Washington over the Lincoln's birthday weekend in 1940. It was not pro-Communist, said Ross, but its Popular Front orientation played into the hands of Red-baiters. The AYC called the president a warmonger, and Mrs. Roosevelt, who addressed the assemblage, detected and deplored a leftist bias. Ross felt MacLeish erred in blaming students for indifference to moral issues and the menace of fascism, but they differed from their elders on how to respond and were overwhelmingly opposed to war. At Williams College, Professor Schuman was denounced for using the lecture hall as a soapbox; the *Daily Kansan,* at Lawrence, reminded the faculty the lives at risk were the students'; at Harvard pickets in gas masks marched outside the classroom of a belligerent professor; and the president of the University of Michigan expelled six leaders of the American Student Union as "troublemakers." Kansas State remained quiet, but Rickel and I observed that among visiting speakers to the campus, pacifists Kirby Page and A. J. Muste attracted the most notice. The famous, or infamous, "Oxford Oath" of the thirties, "I will not bear arms for flag or country," blinded many students to the dangers of fascism.

Reading now the faded and brittle copy of the six-column brochure Rickel and I put together to announce the formation of Democracy's Volunteers, I am awed by the militancy of it. To the groups we hoped to organize on college campuses we gave the name "battalions." We called for conscription of "capital-power" as well as "man-power." We called for a kind of universal service: a national program of youth camps to instill democratic ideas and values, where, taking a leaf from Mumford, "the wisest and best shall be given every educational opportunity in order to perfect a true democratic society." We called also for better protection of the civil rights of racial and social minorities and firm resistance to those who preached hatred and intolerance. A five-hundred–word "Blueprint for Democracy" stated our credo. We believe in democracy, it began, as the most perfect expression of human freedom and dignity. Of course, democracy had its faults, but none that could not be corrected through experience and education. Democracy required a nurturing environment; it could not survive in isolation. "Free peoples must stand together wherever and whenever their liberties are threatened." Democracy also required sacrifice. "The all too common attitude of youth, of callous pacifism, indifference, and inaction must be replaced by one of aggressive militancy, intelligent interest, and zealous labor." Finally, we said, "now is the time to lay the foundations for a just and permanent peace." The brochure included quotations from Jefferson and Paine and flew the slogan, "Democracy Has Just Begun to Fight." We listed a council of advisers, among them Mumford, Lerner, Streit, Fischer, Schuman, and Reinhold Niebuhr, the liberal Protestant theologian. The latter's endorsement was quoted: "I believe in Democracy's Volunteers because our desperate and international problem has been approached with so much sentimentality and illusion, especially on the part of the younger generation, that one is grateful for the combination of realism and idealism which informs this movement."

Alas, it never became a movement. Word of Democracy's Volunteers was picked up by local and regional media and reported in some eastern newspapers as an oddity from the heartland where the America First mentality was supposed to reign. During the next eight or nine months of late 1940 and early 1941, Rickel and I made some speeches in Kansas and corresponded with interested students on a number of campuses, and a handful of chapters were organized. But impact was minuscule, for obvious reasons: we had no money, no staff, no office other than my Manhattan home. Rickel, who was older, finished college in the coming year, and I transplanted myself to Lawrence. After the Soviet Union entered the war against Germany, we thought the United States likely to follow and ultimate victory assured. After the attack on Pearl Harbor, I lost interest in Democracy's Volunteers altogether. Evidently, some fragments of it survived and were absorbed, as I was led to understand, into the consolidated left-liberal American Youth for Democracy.

Leafing through the crumbling pages of old issues of the *New Republic,* I am reminded of the many good things it contained on topics apart from the main event. Nicholas Nabokov wrote on Russian music, especially the brassy Shostakovich. Alistair Cooke, writing on Justice Holmes's death just shy of his one hundredth year, observed, "To complain that Holmes had become a cult is only to say that liberals, leftists, and readers of the *New Republic* recognized a friend in an unlikely field." The justices were not without their critics. In 1941, Edith Abbott, a pioneer of American social work, seized the occasion of the Supreme Court's overturning of the infamous *Hammer v. Dagenhart* (1918) ruling, which had callously protected child labor, to remark smartly that the surviving children exploited in mills and factories should bring suit for damages against the august court for their broken bodies and stunted minds. (Her letter appeared on the correspondence page, always one of the *New Republic*'s best features.) Otis Ferguson's reviews of films and jazz were always lively and informative. He was an early fan of Preston Sturges's movies, and the fact that he took Benny Goodman seriously endeared him to me. I was impressed, too, by drama critic Stark Young and his audacious liking for William Saroyan's plays. An article by Edgar Johnson, an English professor, "Veblen: Man from Mars," was my introduction to this fascinating social satirist. Johnson observed, strikingly, that Sinclair Lewis's novels were "nothing but dramatized Veblen." George West's "The Westbook Pegler Mind" explicated guttersnipe journalism. Edmund Wilson's contributions, while no longer regular, were invariably interesting. In

"Vienna: Idyll and Earthquake," ostensibly a review of Franz Hoelling's *The Defenders: Vienna in 1934,* he attempted to define a new literary form he called "the novel of contemporary history," represented by the works of Malraux, Silone, and Dos Passos, among others. Selections from Wilson's big book on Marxism, *To the Finland Station,* also ran in the magazine's pages.

One of the steps in the *New Republic*'s halting progress toward war was its acceptance, in August, of conscription, or "selective service," which would have been inconceivable in April when "The Corruption of Liberalism" appeared. That same month it published Stanley E. Hyman's stinging profile of Charles Lindbergh, "The Lonely Eagle," the nation's foremost isolationist spokesman. Chronicling the flight of the aviator's fame, Hyman said, "He was hounded by every crank and madman in the country, and after a while Lindbergh came to identify all the American people with the pitiful lunatics." He escaped to Germany only to be seduced by the Third Reich. In 1940 he became the best-known voice of the America First Committee. His wife, Anne Morrow Lindbergh, meanwhile, wrote a best-selling book, *The Wave of the Future,* which predicted fascism's victory and countenanced racism. Dorothy Thompson, the well-known columnist who first blew the whistle on Lindbergh, said he exactly fit the figure of one rehearsing the role of Hitler's American Gauleiter. The *New Republic* agreed, but Walter Lippmann, Thompson's colleague, said he was only naive.

In this department the editors had their own problem child, John T. Flynn, the Wall Street columnist. Readers often remarked upon the gulf between the editors' opinions and those found in Flynn's column, "Other People's Money." He hated the New Deal. His book *Country Squire in the White House* was an ugly election-year portrait of Roosevelt. To this he added Irish animosity to the "sceptered isle." Flynn remembered the days when the magazine blamed war on the bankers and haggled over every dollar spent for arms. Now, he said, it was "Johnny Get Your Gun." One faithful reader, John Haynes Holmes, wondered at the editors' patience and opined that it was Flynn who stood to them as Bourne had in the Great War. Finally, after Flynn rose to leadership in America First and presided at a Madison Square Garden rally, he and his column were dropped. Flynn defended himself, saying he had not changed his political stance in eight years. The editors, on the other hand, had turned somersaults.

The Battle of Britain was won in the summer and fall of 1940. Not that the country was out of danger, but the Royal Air Force (RAF) had prevailed in the air war, and the threat of imminent invasion had passed. Edward R. Murrow, aided by Eric Sevareid and others, had reported the London bombings by radio. Hearing Murrow's velvety voice announcing "This is London," heralded by the booms of Big Ben, was both alarming and reassuring. "This night bombing is serious and sensational. It makes headlines, kills people, and smashes property; but it doesn't win wars." H. N. Brailsford, the veteran correspondent, stroked sympathetic American hearts with a little book called *From England to America: A Message*. The *New Republic* again rejected his pleas for declaration of war before it was too late. Brailsford could describe Britain as "an organization for total war." The United States was still far from that condition. As the months passed, a new note entered Brailsford's reports. The war was producing a social revolution in Britain. The rich could not live as before; tax rates would not permit it. Workers' incomes rose. The roles of women were changing. Class barriers were falling in every sector, most obviously in the armed services. Education and skills were more widely shared. Health care and social services promised improvement. And Hitler might be thanked for forcing Englishmen to plan the rebuilding of London. MacLeish, reviewing J. B. Priestley's latest book, *Out of the People,* called attention to the same changes. What had happened, he said, was that the people were coming together, not in common danger alone, but in the vision of their democratic possibilities. How far-reaching these changes were is conjectural. But Sevareid, in his memoir *Not So Wild a Dream* (1946), made the same point. Under Hitler's guns a new conception of the war took form. "Perhaps we confused the wish with the fact," the newsman wrote, "but we caught sight of a new England; men who so suffered and achieved in common would no longer regard one another's clothes, accents, or manners but would regard one another in terms of true worth. . . . For the first time the war seemed to have taken a positive meaning." It became commonplace in liberal quarters to speak of the war as a revolution: a social-democratic revolution in place of Nazism's "revolution of nihilism."

Bliven, Soule, and company continued to view mobilization of American industry for war production as an instrument of social change. Unfortunately, in early 1941, its progress was painfully slow as Roosevelt enunciated the four freedoms and proposed lend-lease to Congress. Britain and the United States together had not caught up with Germany and occupied Europe in war production. In Germany itself, the editors calculated, one-half of working time was devoted to war production; Britain now approached that, but in the United States only thirty minutes of each eight-hour day was for guns rather than butter. The failure thus far to convert America's industrial might to the war was, of course, a principal reason for the *New Republic*'s stance against belligerency. Everywhere the mistakes of the last war were being repeated. It was "business as usual," which is to say for profit. In May the editors declared, "The country is in the greatest danger in its whole history." It was losing the battle for control of the North Atlantic, and Britain's lifeline, to German submarines. Forty percent of the goods shipped ended up at the bottom of the ocean. "America must shake off this creeping paralysis of will and do it soon or the Battle of the World will be lost."

A bold fireside chat by the president in June revived the editors' confidence. Then, at the month's end, came Germany's surprise attack on the Soviet Union. "One Day That Shook the World" was the resonant title of the lead editorial. With the dissolution of the Nazi-Soviet Pact, the war in Europe suddenly became what it was meant to be from the first: a Popular Front war against fascism. On August 25 the *New Republic* used its cover to call "For a Declaration of War." The lead editorial conceded that prior assumptions had been proven wrong. But the country was unprepared for war, and the betrayal of the

First World War still cast a long shadow. "We were right to hesitate at first. It is no sign of strength to take precipitate action. . . . And it took time," the editors continued, "to understand the true meaning of events, and to be ready both mentally and physically. But now we do understand. And now we are much nearer to being prepared." So much for apology. The question now was, "Can we rise to the level of the greatest crisis our civilization has ever known? It is our privilege to make the history that will furnish the reply."

The editors fidgeted as one provocation after another passed without bringing a declaration of war on Germany. The war finally came to America through the back door, at Pearl Harbor. Like the rest of the country, readers of the *New Republic,* myself among them, were ill-prepared for the Japanese attack. In retrospect, the magazine's skimpy coverage of events in Asia, including Japanese-American diplomacy, is striking. Japan, however, was a member of the Axis, and so its attack on the United States was strategically linked with the war in Europe. War with Japan led inexorably to war with Germany and Italy.

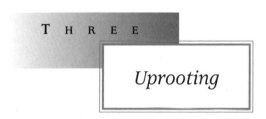

THREE

Uprooting

On December 7, 1941, I was a junior at the University of Kansas (KU), indeed had been enrolled there, and living in Lawrence, since June. I had planned to transfer to KU in any event. Its faculty and curriculum ran more to liberal arts than Kansas State's, and it boasted a department of political science, that esoteric branch of learning I wished to pursue. The move to KU occurred, however, amid circumstances that made it a watershed in my life.

My mother had been running a boardinghouse in Manhattan since 1932 at 1127 Vattier Street, a large, three-story frame house near the campus. Here she "roomed" twenty or more students and fed upward of fifty. Mom had a head for business, but she never kept books—it was all in her head—and the only help came from my brothers and me and the handful of students employed to clean and serve. She had experienced financial problems before, but in 1941 she ran out of wiggle room and was forced to declare bankruptcy. Since she rented the house, she lost only furnishings and equipment, salvaging her considerable dignity and pride.

My leaving for a college eighty miles away thus assumed larger significance. It marked the end to home, to the boardinghouse, the drugstore, to KSAC, friends, and hometown—the things that had counted most in my growing up. And I was not the only one to leave. My family dispersed then, and it would never come together again. Brother Bill had graduated from college three years ago. Discharging his ROTC obligation, he was caught in the army buildup of the Second World War and served for its duration and some years beyond. My brother Ralph, closest to me in age, was started on a career in biology and preparing to go to Brown University for an advanced degree. Mom, too, left Manhattan, stopping first with her brother in Kansas City, then, after some peregrination, she hooked up with a favorite aunt in North Adams, Massachusetts, and found employment as stewardess of a fraternity house at nearby Williams College. In May I threw my books and other belongings together and moved to Lawrence, where I rented a room for six dollars a month on the top floor of a big house on the easterly slope of Mount Oread. The family was thus uprooted from Manhattan. None of us ever returned.

I began my studies that summer and got a job at the grill in the student union. The faculty of the political science department, I discovered, numbered half a dozen. Its chairman, Walter Sandelius, a Rhodes Scholar, taught comparative government and the history of political theory. Carl Friedrich's *Constitutional Government and Democracy* was our text in the former and George H. Sabine's *History of Political Thought* in the latter. Over the next eighteen months, I covered the range of departmental offerings, from U.S. constitutional law to local government and public administration. My principal teacher, and a major influence, was Hilden Gibson, the young star of the department. He was a homegrown product who had gone on to earn his Ph.D. at Stanford University with a dissertation that interpreted Marxism from the standpoint of American pragmatism. (I am reminded of Max Eastman's wisecrack, heard years hence, about Sidney Hook's *Towards the Understanding of Karl Marx,* saying it should be subtitled, "What Karl Marx Would Have Thought Had He Been a Student of John Dewey." The same might have been said of Gibson's dissertation.) Gibson's teaching encompassed recent political theory and American institutions. He seemed to attract the most eager undergraduates and entered into fellowship with them. Under his sway I became a budding Marxist. The big red *Handbook of Marxism,* from International Publishers, was my text. I have always counted this study a valuable educational gain. It introduced me to a fascinating intellectual system, one that gave me a critical vantage point on the society I knew, together with a sense of history that appealed to my hopes for a better world. Happily, I was not imprisoned by it. The hard edges of the ideology soon wore off; nevertheless, Marxism left a permanent imprint on my mind. The dissolution of the Nazi-Soviet Pact had removed the incubus it would otherwise have been under. The penalty for this, however, was a seriously distorted image of Soviet Communism, for Gibson, himself a fellow traveler, introduced me as well to such false and misleading works as Sidney and Beatrice Webb's *The Truth about Soviet Russia* and the then popular but outrageous tract *The Soviet Power,* by Hewlett Johnson, "the Red Dean of Canterbury." As long as the Soviet Union was our gallant ally, I found it hard to form a realistic estimate of Soviet Communism.

Gibson also opened my mind to the gathering stream of writing devoted to the rediscovery of the American past, and this, I came to realize, was more interesting to me than the study of political science. He introduced me to works of American autobiography, most particularly that of Lincoln Steffens. The book gracefully traced the career of the California "Boy on Horseback" who became the greatest of the muckrakers, unveiling "The System" of big-money capitalist power and corruption that poisoned the wellspring of American democracy. Steffens, too, was a fellow traveler, the man who in 1919 had famously declared, from Russia, "I have seen the future; and it works." Gibson put me on to Vernon Louis Parrington's *Main Currents in American Thought,* which offered a liberal Jeffersonian interpretation of the nation's literary tradition. I never had an undergraduate course in American literature, yet tried to read F. O. Matthiessen's *American Renaissance,* published to critical acclaim in 1941. Alfred Kazin's groundbreaking *On Native Grounds* appeared the next year. It began where Parrington left off, and I learned much from it. The last chapter, "America! America!"—a prepublication excerpt appeared in the *New Republic*—was a paean to the literature of American self-discovery. Kazin referred to the rich vein opened by Van Wyck Brooks, Mumford, MacLeish, Constance

Rourke, Carl Sandburg, and such newcomers as Dos Passos. "Suddenly," Kazin wrote, "as if it marked a necessary expiation of too rapid and embittered disillusionment in the past, American writing became a swelling chorus of national affirmation and praise."

Dos Passos was a particularly interesting case of a change of mind about America. From his early "lost generation" novels through the trilogy *U.S.A.,* he had offered a harsh, sad, even cynical view of American character and institutions. The last novel of the trilogy, *The Big Money,* is populated with hollow men and women caught up in the whirl of an acquisitive society. The pathetic young social worker Mary French stands apart from the society, yet is victimized by it. She ends up marching to save Sacco and Vanzetti from the electric chair; and when beaten, she concludes helplessly with the author, "all right we are two nations." Even in this despairing book, however, there is the sense of a great American tradition, a lifeline to the past, to be revivified and renewed. The sacrifice of Sacco and Vanzetti, haters of oppression, whose alleged crime occurred at Plymouth, where the first immigrants landed, was the starting point for reclaiming, in the author's voice, "the ruined words worn slimy in the mouths of lawyers district attorneys college presidents judges." A year or so later, coincident with publication of *Adventures of a Young Man,* Dos Passos applied for, and received, a Guggenheim Fellowship to study early American history and write a book of essays on the origins of freedom and democracy. *The Ground We Stand On,* in 1941—again excerpts appeared in the *New Republic*—was an attempt to locate in the times of Roger

Williams, Benjamin Franklin, and Thomas Jefferson the sources of a distinctly American ideology superseding and making unnecessary current ideologies of Left and Right. It was, the *New York Times Book Review* said, "a testament of faith in America." I read the book that way, though I wasn't quite persuaded by it. The book was the pivot upon which Dos Passos's career turned. He moved from Provincetown to a family estate in Virginia and grew politically conservative. Irving Howe, reviewing a later novel, saw Dos Passos as a textbook case of "the perils of Americanism."

Not long after Pearl Harbor, I learned of a naval officer recruitment program, dubbed V-7, that would enable me to complete my bachelor's degree before entering active service. (I couldn't swim, but in the navy, I figured to shake off the dust of Kansas and see the world.) I went to Kansas City, where I passed the requisite physical examination and promptly registered in the program. Because I was eager to serve in the war, I accelerated my studies and satisfied degree requirements in January 1943.

All the while I continued weekly reading of the *New Republic.* In my retrospective survey of the bound volumes —six months to a fat volume—a number of themes stand out. On the home front, after Pearl Harbor, there was a veneer of national unity that boded well for the conduct of the war. The Harvard historian Arthur M. Schlesinger, after looking at divisions in past wars, concluded with the president, "The Union has never been more closely knit together." The editors were inclined to agree, yet they observed alarming social and political discords. Moreover, the pace of war production lagged behind the demands of grand strategy abroad. Michael Straight, son of the founders, had been added to the editorial board. He set up the magazine's Washington office and employed his lively pen to assay foreign and domestic problems. An early article titled "Dollar-a-Year Sabotage" held that the outcome of the production battle was still in doubt three months after Donald Nelson, a wizard from Sears Roebuck, had been named to head the newly created War Production Board (WPB). This was partly because the corporate executives Nelson recruited continued to draw large salaries from their companies. Straight was scarcely alone in suspecting they placed their companies' interests ahead of the national interest. The procedure, however necessary, made a farce of the antitrust laws. Five years earlier Thurman Arnold, in an eye-opening book, *The Folklore of Capitalism,* had argued that the enforcement of these laws had become little more than a sanctimonious ritual. Now, in an amazing switch, Arnold found himself head of the Justice Department's antitrust division. He persuaded Congress to increase its budget threefold and built up a large staff of trust-busting lawyers just at the time the business went out of fashion. The reporter Richard Lee Strout contributed "The Folklore of Thurman Arnold," an amusing account detailing his misfortunes. As to Nelson, the *New Republic* checked its fears and backed him 100 percent. So, in the main, did Sen. Harry Truman of Missouri, who made a name for himself as chairman of the watchdog Truman Committee. Its blistering report in January 1942 on the administration's failure to put war production in high gear had finally led the president to create the WPB and bring in Nelson.

In March of that year the *New Republic* hosted a dinner in Washington for two hundred leading liberals to celebrate the tenth anniversary of the New Deal. Some wondered if there was much left to celebrate. Social experimentation was necessarily at a halt, though certain wartime imperatives, such as price controls and higher taxation of the well-to-do were in the spirit of the New Deal. In November, the Democrats suffered defeat at the polls, and the Republicans took control of Congress. For six months the *New Republic* had labored to avert this setback. It published a special section, "A Congress to Win the War," on the voting record of every senator and representative on twenty key issues. This was an important innovation in American politics. In October the record was published as *A Voter's Handbook,* wherein the magazine named its favorite candidates in every state and district. They were virtually all Democrats, for isolationism as well as anti–New Dealism persisted in the Republican party.

Protecting the gains and the influence that had been won by organized labor became a test of the New Deal's viability. Here labor's foremost leader, John L. Lewis, performed like the proverbial bull in the china shop. He loathed Roosevelt, deserted him in 1940, and allowed his personal feelings to override organized labor's "no strike" pledge for the duration of the war. A coal crisis was created when half a million miners struck in May 1943, then defied the president's order to return to work, leading the *New Republic* to observe that they showed greater loyalty to Lewis than to the president. C. Wright Mills, a young sociologist, took exception in "The Case for the Coal Miners." Miners' wages had fallen well behind the rising cost of living, he argued. Yet the government, and the magazine, sided with the operators. The editors rejected the slur, then on second thought, conceded the miners' case. "John L. Lewis," they wrote, "is just about the most irritating man on the public scene in America today. He has conducted the coal negotiations more in the spirit of a Roosevelt-hating Republican and an isolationist than as a genuine labor leader." Still, the miners' average wage was 50 percent below that prevailing in comparable trades, and they were essential to American industry. Moreover, the operators' profits had soared. The strike settlement broke the so-called Little Steel formula, intended to stabilize wages. Congress, meanwhile, passed the Smith-Connally anti-strike law, a dagger in the heart of the New Deal.

The damage done to civil liberties had been a principal count in the liberals' indictment of the First World War. This time around, the fundamental guarantees of the Bill of Rights were, on the whole, well protected. The worst offense was the forced internment, after Pearl Harbor, of 110,000 Japanese Americans, two-thirds of them native-born. Carey McWilliams filed an early report on this enormity in the *New Republic*. The editors labeled it "an American Nuremberg Law," then recognized it as a wartime security precaution they could not change. They remained vigilant opponents, however, of the House Un-American Activities Committee headed by Rep. Martin Dies of Texas. The committee, in turn, had the temerity to attack the *New Republic* and its editor, Bruce Bliven, for attempting to subvert republican government. When the inquisitors' axe fell on Robert M. Lovett, a former associate of the magazine, then secretary of the government of the Virgin Islands, the editors denounced the action as "one of the most disgraceful of the last few decades." (The Supreme Court later voided the rider of an appropriations bill that deprived Lovett of his salary, calling it a virtual bill of attainder.) They cheered Dies's decision not to seek reelection in 1944 and hoped that his committee would end up in "the ashcan" of history. Alas, it would be continued under another somewhat less provocative chairman.

The war reawakened interest in the core American race problem: the equal rights of the Negro. The president took an immense stride in 1941 with the issuance of Executive Order 8802, which outlawed discrimination in employment on defense contracts. He acted under the pressing threat of a march on Washington by 50,000 blacks led by A. Philip Randolph, president of the Brotherhood of Sleeping Car Porters. The order established the Fair Employment Practices Committee to secure the goal. It was poorly funded, however, and ran up against the discriminatory practices of trade unions. "Josh White [the folk singer] might well make up a new 'social significance blues' around Executive Order 8802's unfulfilled promise to the Negro," a reporter tracking the experiment wrote early in 1943. That summer there were race riots and rumors of riots from New York to Los Angeles. The worst was in Detroit, the nation's fourth-largest city, swollen with the bigotry of the Klan, Father Coughlin, and Gerald L. K. Smith. "A blind man could see it coming," Thomas Sancton wrote in the *New*

Republic. "There was race hate there older than the Nazi Party, older than the American Constitution." Sancton, the magazine's managing editor, authored a series of eyewitness reports, "Trouble in Dixie," that related rising racial tensions to southern "secession" from the New Deal. He picked up the rumor of so-called Eleanor Clubs, the first lady being the most hated woman in the South since Harriet Beecher Stowe, that supposedly agitated among black household servants. "The Negro: His Future in America," a supplement published in October, noted reason for encouragement. Membership in the National Association for the Advancement of Colored People was rising steadily, some two hundred interracial committees had been organized in American cities, and in 1944, in Atlanta, a group of interracial leaders organized the Southern Regional Council committed to militant leadership. Old problems like poll taxes and lynchings festered without legislative relief. A favorable straw in the wind was the Supreme Court's decision abolishing the white primary in the South.

What I, along with the *New Republic*, failed to appreciate at this time was the irony that the social and economic reforms legislated by the Roosevelt Coalition exacted the price of acquiescence in the South's peculiar arrangements for the Negro. The same Democratic votes that helped to enact New Deal measures, including those leading to war, also blocked antilynching and anti–poll tax legislation and sustained the reign of Jim Crow. The price of liberal reform, in some sense, was paid by black Americans. Education in these matters had barely begun.

A small flood of books on the Negro appeared during the war. There was J. Saunders Redding's *No Day of Triumph,* an impressionistic account of the southern black man; Roi Ottley's *"New World a Coming,"* with its focus on Harlem; and *Black Metropolis,* a landmark sociological study of Chicago's blacks by St. Clair Drake and Horace Cayton. Every one of these books recognized that racial insult and discrimination was a war issue, affecting not just U.S. citizens but peoples around the world. The Negro's cause, as Ottley said, was "the barometer of democracy." Not to be overlooked were the best-selling novel *Strange Fruit,* by a white activist from Georgia, Lillian Smith, and Richard Wright's moving memoir of his childhood, *Black Boy.*

But the most important work was authored neither by an American nor by a Negro. This was *An American Dilemma: The Negro Problem and Modern Democracy,* in 1944, by the Swedish social scientist Gunnar Myrdal, whose exhaustive six-year study had been commissioned by the Carnegie Corporation. In the first chapter of his monumental work, Myrdal, from his European vantage point, observed that all Americans, regardless of race or national origin, of religion, class, or region, profess basically identical social and political ideals and share a common ethos and that this "American Creed" is the real cement of this great and disparate nation. "America, compared to every other country in Western civilization, large or small, has the most explicitly expressed system of general ideals in reference to human interrelationships. This body of ideals is more widely understood and appreciated than similar ideals are anywhere else." Myrdal located the premier statement of the creed in the nation's founding document, the Declaration of Independence. To be sure, the creed was not satisfactorily effectuated, as witnessed by the Negro problem. "But as principles that ought to rule, the Creed has been made conscious to everyone in American society." Myrdal maintained that one reason so little social progress had been made in attacking the problem was the outmoded rubric of the social sciences that "stateways cannot change folkways," and he called for affirmative national action to do precisely that. I first became aware of *An American Dilemma* through the favorable review appearing in the *New Republic,* and its postulates entered deeply into everything I later thought and wrote about America.

The *New Republic* telescoped war aims into postwar aims. If the war was to be a democratic revolution, it had to be infused with democratic actions and goals. Henry Luce, publisher of *Life,* in a celebrated editorial, "The American Century," envisioned the war as a pax Americana. Max Lerner, in response, recognized this as an important statement and agreed upon the future leadership role of the United States; but Luce's conception bristled with imperial capitalist conceit, such as was to be expected from a man who had fought the New Deal for eight years. The best answer to Luce came in a widely publicized address by Vice President Henry A. Wallace in May 1942. The world of tomorrow must not be "an American century," he declared, but "the century of the common man," guided by the light of the president's four freedoms. Some months later the crucial document of British postwar planning, the Beveridge Report, part 1, appeared in the United States. The work of the English don and government servant William Beveridge, it laid out a comprehensive system of social security, "from the cradle to the grave," for all citizens. (The second part, *Full Employment in a Free Society,* was published to like acclaim in 1944.) Bliven and company promptly called for "A Beveridge Plan for America." The need was urgent. One of the startling disclosures of selective service was that of the first two million young Americans of draft age tested, almost half were physically or mentally unfit. Something on the order of an American Beveridge Report came from a little-known government agency, the National Resources Planning Board (NRPB). It looked to improved social security benefits, improved housing, health care, and education, and also to full employment backed by compensatory public spending. "What it amounts to is the social service state," Lerner wrote with glee. The *New York Times,* on the other hand, denounced the report. Of course, the chances of a Republican Congress acting on it were nil. Roosevelt understood this. As Bliven wrote discouragingly of the NPRB report, "he gingerly left it as a May basket on Congress's doorstep, rang the bell and ran away."

Things went better internationally. Something called the United Nations, of which I was scarcely aware at the time, was struggling to be born. Announced at the beginning of 1942, having been approved by Roosevelt and Churchill, it was an alliance of the United States, Great Britain, China, the USSR, and twenty-two other countries at war with the Berlin-Rome-Tokyo Axis. It included two-thirds of the world's people, and while conceived in war, it was dedicated to building an enduring peace. A number of books appeared on the foundations of and the shape to be given this new world order. Among the first was *Conditions of Peace* by British scholar Edward H. Carr. The *New Republic*'s own Michael Straight, soon to enter the air force, weighed in with *Make This the Last War*. Apropos of the relationship between the war and the peace, Straight observed "that when the Nazis hammer Europe into their economy, they are creating the permanent structure of the New Order . . . the basis for a United Europe." And he exclaimed, "Never has there been such an opportunity." Nothing equaled the popular influence of Wendell Willkie's *One World* in 1943. It sold over a million copies in the United States alone. An interventionist Republican, Willkie had put himself at the president's disposal after Pearl Harbor, and Roosevelt sent him around the world in an air force bomber as his personal emissary of global peace and order. To all this, though more specifically to Henry Wallace, Clare Boothe Luce, the freshman Republican congresswoman from Connecticut, scoffed "globaloney."

The *New Republic*'s coverage of the Asian theater continued to be thin. Then in 1942 the magazine's attention was caught by the extraordinary mission of Sir Stafford Cripps to India with a plan of self-government that would enlist the country in the war. Since the disastrous loss of Singapore to the Japanese in February, fears were rife of invasion of India through Burma and the isolation of the Chinese government in Chungking. There was also the danger that Indian nationalists, impatient with their imperial masters, would join the Japanese. About this

time I was reading *Toward Freedom,* the autobiography of
Jawaharlal Nehru. Robert Lovett had reviewed the work
in the *New Republic.* It became a favorite book, inspiring
my interest in India and making Nehru a personal hero.
Who could not, with an attraction to matters of history
and character, but be fascinated by the study of the two
great Indian leaders, Mohandas Gandhi and Nehru, one
a saint, a Mahatma, the other a modern intellectual, a
democrat, and a socialist? They represented two poles,
East and West. Nehru was not of one, yet felt an exile in
the other. He only went along with Gandhi's program of
communalism and nonviolence; it worked when nothing
else would, and borrowing from William James, Nehru
called it "the moral equivalent of war." Half of the twenty-
two years he had given to the movement for Indian independence had been spent in prison. "It is one of the
tragic ironies of the present world situation," wrote a
Far East specialist in the *New Republic,* "that the United
Nations can find no better way to use one of the great
pro-democratic thinkers and statesmen in Asia than to
immobilize him in prison."

The Cripps mission failed for a number of reasons,
but mainly, as Nehru said, because the British offer did
not meet the essential Indian condition of immediate
freedom and unity of its people. The Englishman seemed
amazed by the refusal, and he responded, "You don't
mean you really want to break away from us entirely,
do you?" Such was the gulf between them.

Pearl Buck, lamenting the defeat in a speech before
Nobel Prize winners in New York, said that we must
get over the idea that war is waged to save Western

civilization. "It will be out of the Far East, out of India, and out of China, that our civilization will be reborn," just as at an earlier time rebirth came from the East. "The roots of human civilization are in Asia, not in Europe," she intoned. If this was strident, it was meant for those, like Churchill, imprisoned by the imperial past, and like Clarence Streit, who would build the new order on the narrow foundation of Western democracies. H. N. Brailsford, in his fine analysis of the crisis, *Subject India,* chose to end on a philosophical note, borrowed from the conclusion of E. M. Forster's *A Passage to India.* In the novel, the two friends, the Indian Aziz and the Englishman Fielding, go on a last ride together. The talk recurs to politics. Aziz boasts of eventually ridding the country of " 'every blasted Englishman . . . and then,' he concluded, half-kissing him, 'you and I shall be friends.' 'Why can't we be friends now?' " Fielding asks. " 'It's what I want. It's what you want.' " The author continues: "But the horses didn't want it—they swerved apart; the earth didn't want it, sending up rocks through which riders must pass single file . . . 'No, not yet,' and the sky said, 'No, not there.' "

As military prospects brightened in 1943, and Allied statesmen met with increasing frequency on the structure of the peace, Congress fumbled its way toward commitment to a permanent international organization. In September the House passed the Fulbright Resolution to this end; the process culminated in the Senate's adoption six weeks later of the Connally Resolution. (J. William Fulbright was then an Arkansas representative; Tom Connally, of Texas, was chairman of the Senate

Foreign Relations Committee.) The *New Republic* cheered the passage, saying it sounded the death knell of isolationism and repudiated the rejection of the League of Nations in 1920. One of the rejectionists, Hiram Johnson of California, still sat in the Senate. T. R. B., the magazine's unnamed Washington political columnist, wrote movingly of the seventy-nine-year-old senator rising to his feet and, in a scarcely audible voice, uttering "a broken choked prayer for America, joining a minute later with four others—Wheeler, Reynolds, Langer and Shipstead—in the minority of the 85-to-5 vote passing the amended Connally Resolution." The resolution, appropriately vague, had no binding effect; yet it marked the end of the old order of isolationism.* Public opinion polls showed that the American people overwhelmingly endorsed an international organization dominated by the victorious powers. The pace of planning for it picked up.

What little knowledge I had during the war of the Nazi atrocity against the Jews, later to be named the Holocaust, I got from the *New Republic*. In retrospect, I realize it was meagerly reported even there. In December 1942, several months after news of the extermination camps had reached the West, the magazine published a forthright editorial called "The Massacre of the Jews."

---

*T. R. B. was presumably Richard Lee Strout, Washington reporter for the *Christian Science Monitor.* Why the editors kept the author's name a secret always puzzled me. Bliven, in his autobiography, said the pseudonymous initials were a last-minute invention of his, T. R. B. being the reverse of the abbreviation for Brooklyn Rapid Transit, which gave subway access to the printing plant in lower Manhattan.

Upon the authority of Rabbi Stephen S. Wise, it confirmed reports that some one million Polish Jews had been killed, and the Germans seemed bent on annihilating the race as the first object of the war. The reports were almost too incredible to be believed, the editors observed, but they could not be dismissed as "atrocity-mongering." This was quickly followed by an in-house article that raised the estimate of the slain to two million. The Nazis could not be judged by civilized standards, the author said; he called on the president to speak out and also lift the bar to Jewish refugees. He did neither, unfortunately. By August 1943, when the magazine published a "The Jews of Europe: How to Help Them" as a special section, at least three million, almost half of the Jews on the continent, were dead. Early in the new year the editors applauded Roosevelt's belated action in establishing the War Refugee Board. It actually saved Jewish lives.

As the presidential election of 1944 rolled around, the *New Republic* continued its support of President Roosevelt in his bid for a fourth term. Yet that support had been sorely tried; for instance, there was the appeasement of Admiral Darlan and Vichy France, which finally ended, to the grim relief of many at the magazine, with Darlan's assassination. This, in turn, reflected Roosevelt's deference to an overly cautious State Department under Cordell Hull. In domestic matters, the *New Republic* was angered by Roosevelt's flagging confidence in Vice President Wallace. Wallace, the dedicated New Dealer out of Iowa, had become the liberal standard-bearer in the administration. The president had named him chairman of the Board of Economic Warfare (BEW), which was concerned with strategic materials to fight the war and with long-range policies to further global prosperity. Wallace aimed for a kind of international New Deal. When jurisdictional conflicts arose with the State Department and, more particularly, with Jesse Jones, secretary of commerce and longtime loan czar of the administration, the president abolished the BEW and transferred its authority to an agency under Jones's control. Wallace licked his wounds but kept faith with Roosevelt, saying "Though he slay me, yet will I trust him." Bliven excoriated the president in an editorial titled "Mr. Wallace Walks the Plank." The demotion of Wallace was "the most severe shock to [Roosevelt's] liberal followers since he has been in office, with the possible exception of his negative aid to Franco during the Spanish Civil War." Bliven found the same consolation as Wallace, however.

Archibald MacLeish, always sensitive to the liberals' pulse, expressed his discouragement at a dinner honoring Freda Kirchwey for twenty-five years with the *Nation:* "Liberals meet in Washington these days, if they can endure to meet at all, to discuss the tragic outlook for all liberal proposals, the collapse of all liberal leadership and the inevitable defeat of liberal aims. It is no longer feared, it is assumed, that the country is headed back to normalcy, that Harding is just around the corner." The *New Republic* thought this unduly defeatist, despite the sour mood in liberal quarters. Even Reinhold Niebuhr, whose theology steeled him against perfectionism, confessed that Roosevelt was no longer an effective instrument of progressive politics but had no idea of who might replace him. Roosevelt himself, upon his return from Teheran in

December, said the New Deal was no longer the standard of his administration. "Dr. Win-the-War" had replaced "Dr. New Deal." Like Churchill, he was a warrior, first and last; and beyond the platitudinous four freedoms he never entertained the liberal idea that the war was a social revolution.

The Wallace debacle played out at the Democratic National Convention in Chicago in 1944. Never popular with southern Democrats, Wallace had acquired new enemies for his "globaloney." Roosevelt lacked the strength and the will to fight for his renomination. As the campaign to dump him became manifest, the *New Republic* pleaded, "Keep Vice President Wallace," and defined this as the great issue before the convention. Roosevelt, it went on to say, was a compromiser to his fingertips. And determined not to repeat Wilson's mistake in 1920, he required the stiffening rod of Wallace's progressivism. But Wallace was defeated, the magazine lamented, "by all the worst elements of the Democratic Party—the corrupt big city machines . . . [and] the Southern Tories." The successful candidate, Harry Truman of Missouri, was "a good man," T. R. B. wrote. "He will make a passable Vice President. But Truman as President in times like these?"—this was a gasping thought. A week later, Bliven said that Wallace's defeat was, in effect, the epitaph of the New Deal. Ironically, the Supreme Court, with its increasingly liberal opinions, was the only Washington institution to retain "the coloration of the New Deal." After this, the election was an anticlimax.

Darrell Zanuck's motion picture *Wilson,* a hymn to internationalism, was showing at the time of the election.

And internationalism would be the theme of the new year. The Dumbarton Oaks Conference, ending in October, had laid the basis of the postwar United Nations organization, and most of the matters still unsettled were resolved by the Big Three at Yalta in February. The United Nations charter was adopted at the San Francisco Conference in June, after President Roosevelt's death. The work went forward with virtually no dissent from the *New Republic.* Its first special supplement on the Far East appeared in May, two weeks after V-E Day. It did not forecast any special alertness to events in that part of the world, however. The magazine was more attentive to the reconversion of the American economy to peacetime. The editors fought for retention of price controls, lifting of wage controls, and, unsuccessfully, for the excess profits tax. In these matters President Truman got a satisfactory grade after making allowance for a refractory Congress. Irving Brant, formerly a reporter for the *St. Louis Star Times,* who had a close knowledge of the Missourian's political background, contributed his candid assessment two weeks after Truman took the oath of office. Truman was a good man, fairly liberal, colorless but likable, a shrewd and skillful politician, and a team player. T. R. B., looking at the record after six months, had little to add to that: "Truman was a well-intentioned, politically minded middle-roader of higher caliber than some feared and of weaker leadership than some hoped."

The *New Republic* watched anxiously for rifts among the Big Three. By June it was lamenting Roosevelt's absence as a mediator with Stalin. Truman, lacking his experience and finesse, depended on the advice of Secretary of State Edward Stettinius, himself a weak rod, and the anti-Soviet bloc in the department. Every rift was seized upon by forces seeking to embroil the United States and the Soviet Union in conflict. Bliven chastised journalist William E. White for writing a wholly negative eyewitness report on the Russians, one that belonged nowhere but in the pages of the *Reader's Digest*. Churchill had resumed his old hostility to Russia. He traveled to Greece to take a hand in the restoration of the monarchy and the defeat of the popular party, EAM, and its guerilla counterpart, ELAS, which the prime minister charged was Communist. Heinz Eulau, the *New Republic*'s reporter, wrote: "What is happening in Greece is a counterrevolution against a phantom revolution which existed solely in Mr. Churchill's imagination. . . . Greece is temporarily a British colony." Occurring not long before the 1945 general election in Britain, this affair exhibited Churchill to the public in the light of a rank Tory. The Labor Party won a resounding victory: a two-to-one majority in the Commons, and its leader, Clement Attlee, became prime minister. Vincent Sheean, after a long absence, contributed "Valediction to Churchill" to the magazine's pages. He noted that Churchill had been a great leader in war, but he was not made for the quieter ways of peace, nor did he understand the hopes and aspirations of ordinary people. He had outlived his usefulness and become "a toothache" to the world. T. R. B., reflecting on the British election, observed that the United States was the last and only major power wedded to social and economic conservatism, the only one that rejected government to meet the essential needs of the people, the only one where

Frederick Hayek's little book *The Road to Serfdom* was a bestseller.

Following the ideological combat of the thirties, the cultural front grew comparatively quiet, at least in the pages of the *New Republic*. In 1943 Moscow pronounced the Comintern officially dead—deader than the New Deal —and the American Communist Party faced a bleak future. Malcolm Cowley, reviewing four new books about Russia, said it was no longer a revolutionary country. Resurgent Russian nationalism had eclipsed the Bolshevik Revolution. The nation was reborn in the myth of the Great Patriotic War. Thus a war poster featured the likeness of Kutuzov, conqueror of Napoleon, with a legend from Stalin: "Let the valorous example of our great ancestors inspire you in the war." On the Left, disillusionment together with recantation of communism was a sign of the times in the West. Cowley thoughtfully reviewed Arthur Koestler's *Darkness at Noon,* a book that became a classic of the literature, upon its American publication. Being then in my Marxist phase, I was loath to read this novel until several years later. It owed its impact to the Hungarian-born author's brilliant fusion of his own communist identity with that of the protagonist, Rubashov, wrongfully convicted in a staged Moscow trial, yet forced at the depths of his being to recognize his guilt according to the ethic he had professed. Rubashov is finally executed in prison for a faith he no longer believes in. Cowley, while admiring the novel, felt that it was written in the bitterness of disillusion and failed to distinguish between the sins of Stalinism and the sins of Nazism.

Another take on this theme was a review by Granville Hicks, a repentant American Communist from the thirties, of Max Lerner's *Public Journal*. Lerner, although he occasionally contributed to the *New Republic,* had joined *PM,* a brave new experiment in liberal journalism, as an editorial writer. The book collected a hundred of these pieces from the newspaper. As if settling an old score, Hicks picked an argument with Lerner over some criticism of Koestler. The price of the author's expiation of the guilt of communism, Lerner had said, was encouragement of the reactionaries' attacks on liberals. But that argument was a diversion, Hicks insisted. Lerner, with most liberals, seemed more concerned about the consequences of ideas than with their truth or falsity. On Russia, in particular, Hicks said, Lerner's "mind snapped shut some time back." The editors were indignant over the personal asperity of the review, and in the next issue they took the unusual step of responding. Apparently, they argued, Hicks had shed his old faith without shedding the frame of mind that brought him to it in the first place, that is, he saw everything as black or white and wanted all or nothing. And so, unlike liberals such as Lerner and themselves, he was incapable of treating problems close at hand and doing his best with murky options.

Cowley was always quick to defend the literary generation he represented: the exiles of the twenties who came to flourish in the thirties. In 1944, Bernard De Voto, a *Harper's* columnist, published *The Literary Fallacy,* which continued the line of criticism MacLeish had opened with *The Irresponsibles.* The "fallacy" of the title was that literature is a true measure of the culture, and it proved devastating when the masters of the Third Reich read Hemingway, Faulkner, and Dos Passes and concluded that American culture was decadent. Cowley enjoyed making mincemeat of this idea. Similarly with the poetry of Robert Frost, one of De Voto's literary friends. In a two-part essay, the critic filed a dissenting opinion on the man who was rapidly becoming an American icon. At his best, Frost was a good poet, Cowley acknowledged, but, regrettably, he imagined himself a social philosopher in verse and the voice of Yankee tradition. "I have none the tenderer-than-thou / Collectivistic regimented love / With which the modern world is swept." Words like these were inscribed on the banners of right-wing political crusades. "Instead [of being depicted as a poet]," said Cowley, "Frost is depicted by his admirers as a sort of Sunday-school paragon, a saint among miserable sinners." He had become "the Calvin Coolidge of poetry." As much as I admired Frost's poetry, I recognized the truth of Cowley's criticism.

During the war, the *New Republic* printed many poems submitted by servicemen. Few of them were memorable, yet the work of two fine young poets, both servicemen, did turn up in the magazine's pages. One was Karl Shapiro, author of the Pulitzer Prize–winning *V-Letter and Other Poems* in 1944. Another was Selden Rodman who, training at home, addressed his own V-letter to Shapiro in Australia. He flourished their shared hope of America as the land of promise but bewailed "the loud boredom of a thousand barracks" where there was neither "love nor hate, vision of world state nor immaculate village." Much of the verse evoked by the war was excessively sentimental or didactic. Babette Deutch, a poet and critic, tackled the problem in "The Poets and the War"—the specific case of the larger issue of the poet as civic voice—wherein she analyzed Edna St. Vincent Millay's "Murder at Lidice" as an instance of what not to do. Another face of the difficulty showed itself in John Steinbeck's *The Moon is Down,* which was first a short novel and then a Broadway play, set in Nazi-occupied Norway. Steinbeck knew nothing of Norway firsthand. James Thurber panned the book, to the dismay of many readers, though the play fared better in Stark Young's eyes and lifted the spirits of resistance fighters in Europe.

The Broadway stage existed for me only in imagination, of course. Young impressed me with his craftsmanlike intelligence. His sympathies were wide and generous enough to encompass *Antigone* and *Othello, Watch on the Rhine* and *Oklahoma!* His review of Mae West's *Catherine Was Great* was an instant classic. West wrote and starred in the burlesque of the lustful empress, and it was lavishly produced by Mike Todd. What made it entertaining was Miss West's style, Young wrote soberly, which was "strictly presentational." This means "that she finally presents herself and the dramatic moment as herself, as theater, as a show." She has made herself a larger-than-life comedic presence, Young said, "a howling, diverting mythology of glamour."

Otis Ferguson continued to review the movies until he enlisted in the merchant marine in 1942, and he met his death within the year on the Murmansk run. He was succeeded by Manny Farber, who lacked Ferguson's vigorous style but was informative and a pleasure to read. He had a knack for encapsulating his response to a film in a word. For *Casablanca* it was "Hokum," which was not as averse to the critical judgment in December 1942 as it is today; for the Paramount film of the Hemingway novel *For Whom the Bell Tolls,* it was "Tinkle"; for *The Ox-Bow Incident* a rare "Magnificent." For the motion picture made from Ambassador Joseph Davies's Throttlebottomish memoir, *Mission to Moscow,* Farber required two words, "dullest imaginable," adding that "a while ago it was Red-baiting, now is it Red-praising in the same sense, ignorantly." Farber, like his predecessor, was a fan of motion picture director Preston Sturges. He thought *Miracle of Morgan's Creek,* with Betty Hutton and Eddie Bracken, his funniest film. So did I. A high-voltage girl named Trudy Kockenlocker becomes pregnant with no known father in sight, and when she delivers sextuplets claims a down-at-the-socks soldier for the part.

Laughter in any form was hard to come by in the *New Republic.* One week in 1943 the mail bag produced an open letter from Henry Miller, the controversial author. An expatriate in France during the thirties, Miller had returned to America and settled in Big Sur when war broke out. He wrote to say that, although an author by trade, his writing offended against American prudery and no publisher would touch it. So, he averred, he had as much chance of surviving as "a sewer rat." A Sunday painter, he had resorted to selling his watercolors. He would happily offer them on the cheap to *New Republic* readers. To which he added disarmingly: "I would also be grateful for old clothes, shirts, socks, etc. I am 5 feet 8 inches tall, weight 150 pounds, 15½ neck, 38 chest, 32 waist, hat and shoes both size 7 to 7½. Love corduroys." The magazine later reported that the appeal had met with a warm response.

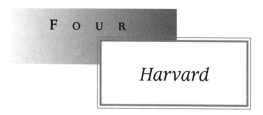

F O U R

Harvard

The course of my life had changed significantly during these years, and it is time to catch up with the changes. After completing my undergraduate studies in January 1943, I bought a one-way ticket by rail to North Adams, Massachusetts. My mother had gone there to reside with her Aunt Mame, and I meant to stay with them until I received orders to report for navy training. Mom worked in a fraternity house at Williams College, only five miles away. I found a job on the night shift of the grill in a downtown hotel and was free in the daytime for other activities, including roving the Williams campus. About the college I knew only that Max Lerner and Frederick Schuman, two of my intellectual idols, taught there. Somehow I wormed my way as a transient observer into courses taught by each of them. The students for Schuman's class in international politics filled a hall. He lectured almost exclusively and in masterly fashion. Lerner's class was smaller, composed, I believe, of upperclassmen. The subject, as far as I could discern, was contemporary American politics, and he engaged the students in easygoing discussion. He was just then winding up his career at Williams, as I later learned, and his mind seemed to be on *PM,* for which he was already writing, and New York City.

In April I received orders to report to Northwestern University, Chicago, to commence training. A former hotel on the lakefront had been converted into a training facility called Tower Hall. All of us in the V-7 program began as apprentice seamen, aiming in the end to be commissioned ensigns in line-officer service. Very soon, however, I learned of an opportunity to transfer into the supply corps by way of a choice new educational program that featured a full year at the Harvard Graduate Business School in Cambridge, Massachusetts. Thrilled by the opportunity, I applied and was accepted. So I returned to the Bay State, this time to the south bank of the Charles River. The business school had pretty much shut down for the duration of the war; however, there was still a small corps of faculty to be kept busy, and the supply corps program may have been developed for that purpose. Certainly, the equivalent of one academic year of graduate business school education exceeded the needs of junior officers. The class numbered about 125, and we lived in the redbrick residence halls along the river. Unlike many of my classmates, I did not aspire to a career in business and so was not seriously engaged by the courses. But they introduced me to the "case method" of instruction—the school's trademark—and I found that challenging. (Many of my classmates returned to the school after the war and picked up MBAs in a single year. I am always amused when something comes in the mail to remind me that I, too, am an alumnus of HGBS.)

By the time we were commissioned in May 1944, the navy had so many supply corps officers that they began to assign them, including most of my class, to destroyer escorts and other small vessels for the first time.

Not long after we arrived, one of the class, a recent graduate of the college, showed us around Harvard Square and the Yard. The place, from all its associations, literary and historical, had a certain magic, and I, with the feelings of an outlander, wished very much to enter. Boston, too, so easily reached by subway from the Square, was wonderful. After a time I learned of Harvard's special Ph.D. program in the history of American civilization. Still very young, it was a forerunner of the American studies movement that came to fruition in the academy after the war. The course of my education had enforced the conviction that the democratic future in America depended, in some part, upon a better understanding and appropriation of the nation's past. This was the lesson of Dos Passos's *The Ground We Stand On;* it was the theme of Parrington's *Main Currents;* it ran through the books of Lewis Mumford and Van Wyck Brooks; it was implicit in Matthiessen's *American Renaissance* and Ralph Gabriel's *Course of American Democratic Thought,* books I first read in college. It was the coda of Kazin's *On Native Grounds.* Having started in 1941 to study political science, I found myself on the track of something quite different, something interdisciplinary, something I later learned had a name, "the search for a usable past" in American history and letters. Luckily, I had willy-nilly arrived at a distinguished university that offered a doctoral program in the field. In the fall I made a visit across the river for an interview with the program's wartime custodian, Benjamin F. Wright, a political scientist, and arranged to apply with the intent of beginning my studies when peace returned.

About the same time, I traveled to New York on leave to visit Mom, who had taken a job as a sort of house-and-home manager with a family there, and also my brother Ralph, who was studying to be a physician, courtesy of the U.S. Army, at Columbia University Medical School–Presbyterian Hospital. (My oldest brother was in North Africa or Italy.) There I was introduced to Jean Humphrey, a tall, good-looking brunette just my age, who became my bride the following May. (On our first date Jean and I went to a new movie, *The Constant Nymph, * with Charles Boyer and Joan Fontaine. It was appropriately romantic and had been reviewed that week in the *New Republic.*) Happily for our courtship, Jean soon moved to Boston to pursue an advanced degree in social work and thereafter settled in Cambridge. And so the pieces of my adult life rapidly fell together.

Commissioned an ensign in the supply corps in May 1944, I was ordered to take a troopship to Recife, Brazil, and report for duty to the USS *Herzog, * DE 178. That duty was abruptly ended, however, when the navy decided to transfer the ship, together with its patrol area in South Atlantic waters, to the Brazilian navy. I returned to the United States on unexpected leave, to a second honeymoon with my wife, after which I reported to the USS *Parle, * DE 708, then being commissioned in Boston. After shakedown the *Parle* briefly saw convoy duty in the Atlantic and Mediterranean, then sailed for the South

Pacific. Captained by "Whitey" Toft, an affable academy graduate, the *Parle* was in the rearguard of the ships island-hopping to Japan. Its guns were never fired in battle. I felt cheated of combat experience. We were in more danger from the weather—a couple of typhoons—than from the enemy. I was never free of mal de mer. Reading was a blessed avocation. Throughout my tour of duty, I bunked with Herb Golden, a New Yorker, who in peacetime was a reporter for *Variety.* Our news came via radio. I remember the shock that ran through the vessel when we heard of President Roosevelt's death, though at that distance it was impossible to enter into the sadness of the occasion. I remember, too, the day the atom bomb exploded on Hiroshima, and I thought at once that such a weapon must be placed under international control. My reading of the *New Republic* became, like the mail, somewhat irregular. Once, we received a large quantity of water-damaged mail that had survived a typhoon in the Ryukus. It included a copy of Auden's *Collected Poems,* sent by my wife, that is still in my library. Sometime after the Japanese surrender, the *Parle* was sent to waters off Seoul, Korea, and there we remained until ordered home to Boston in December. My discharge was dated January 21, 1946.

I was no sooner reunited with Jean, in Cambridge, than I was able to begin graduate work in American civilization at Harvard. When I had applied for graduate study, I had no idea of how to pay for it. But like many returning servicemen in the between-the-wars generation, I was the beneficiary of the GI Bill, the wisest legislation of Congress respecting education since the Land Grant

College Act. The professor of English who became my adviser, Perry Miller, had been in the Office of Strategic Services and still wore his officer's uniform. I knew nothing about him. He did not enroll me in any course he was to teach the coming semester. Of course, I quickly learned that Miller was Harvard's preeminent scholar of New England Puritanism. I was not strongly attracted to that subject. In the following summer session, I enrolled in Miller's course on American romanticism, which gave me the first keen, clear sense of academic study in the field I had entered and, more particularly, of the history of ideas in America. I liked the course and, fortunately, Miller liked the work I submitted and invited me to become a grading assistant in his undergraduate American literature survey in the fall. This boosted my confidence. I never looked back after that, though I had very little idea of what lay ahead of me.

The strength of the Harvard program, I came to realize, was in American literature. It was, in fact, an outgrowth of a successful undergraduate major in American history and literature. The leadership came from Americanists in the English department: Kenneth Murdoch, chairman, Matthiessen, Miller, and Howard Mumford Jones. There was an equivalent constellation of stars in American history—Samuel Eliot Morison, A. M. Schlesinger, Frederick Merk, and young Oscar Handlin. They were less involved in the program, however. And there were political scientists like Wright and his young colleague Louis Hartz; the distinguished philosopher Ralph Barton Perry, whose history of American philosophy course I was able to catch in his retirement year; and scattered faculty in related fields. Nothing was offered to help the student bring the various disciplines together in some unified conspectus of American civilization. The idea, rather, was to encourage the student to view any subject of inquiry from multiple perspectives and to enrich understanding through the interaction. The model study, though, in truth, there were no models, appeared in 1950: *Virgin Land: The American West as Symbol and Myth,* by Henry Nash Smith, who was among the first graduates of the program. That work, which totally recast thinking about the West in the American imagination, could not then have been written in an English or a history department and so was a powerful justification of the American studies approach. Since no one could attain true multidisciplinary competency, and since American universities were structured to discrete disciplines, students in the program gravitated inevitably toward a single discipline, ordinarily history or literature. At Harvard most chose the latter; I, on the other hand, gravitated to history.

Candidates for the Ph.D. in American civilization were required to take two research seminars. As it happened, neither of my choices had a significant bearing on my subsequent scholarship. In one, Carl Friedrich's seminar in modern political theory, I wrote my paper on the late-eighteenth-century English radical William Godwin. In the other, under Oscar Handlin, the social historian and student of immigration, I wrote a paper on "The I. W. W. [the Wobblies] and the Immigrants." It turned out to be a promising subject, well worthy of investigation, and had I chosen to pursue it, I would have entered the track of social or perhaps labor history. That was a road not taken, however; the real benefit of the seminar to me came from Handlin's careful reading of my paper and his blue-pencil comments. For the first time I was made to think seriously about writing.

When it came time to select a dissertation topic, I reverted to an idea that first occurred to me in Miller's course on romanticism. He had talked of the eulogies of Adams and Jefferson in 1826 as a defining American moment and also of the way George Bancroft, the first historian of the United States, had "romanticized" Jefferson's ideas. Under Wright's guidance, I did independent reading on Jefferson, continuing an interest sparked by Parrington. Arthur M. Schlesinger, Jr., had just published *The Age of Jackson* to critical acclaim. Indeed, a 30,000–word abridgement ran serially in the *New Republic*. With my G. I. Bill book allowance I purchased a copy. The work created intellectual excitement around the era. I thought it would be interesting to pursue the way Americans had thought and written about Jefferson through time—a sort of myth and symbol study—and I had the wit to seize upon the word *image,* which was entering the vocabulary, to describe the historical phenomenon. And so, after passing my general examination for the degree early in 1948, I submitted to Miller the prospectus for a dissertation entitled "The Jefferson Image in the American Mind." Miller laid no claim to authority on Jefferson, but he immediately grasped the idea. Not only had I come to regard him as a mentor, but he was easily the best American intellectual historian around. He agreed to supervise the dissertation. In the caverns of Widener Library I began my research. That summer I journeyed to the Library of Congress and the University of Virginia in pursuit of it.

Looking back I am amazed by how innocent I was about things academic, beginning with the potential significance of the doctoral dissertation for one's career, for instance, its bearing on publication, hence promotion and tenure in a college or university. My dissertation did not lend itself to a quick book. It ran, embarrassingly, to one thousand pages in typescript, and with that I had only reached the year 1865. I might have published the result, much condensed, as a monograph. But to do so would have been to sacrifice the sweep and force of the theme. I chose to take the narrative to the present. A decade passed before *The Jefferson Image in the American Mind* was published. It proved to be the turning point in my career.

FIVE

Mind-Shapers

About the time I began reading the *New Republic,* the magazine was running a series of essays called "Books That Changed Our Minds." Malcolm Cowley and Bernard Smith, a leftist critic, collected them into a volume, which was published under the same title. It was a exercise in what Edmund Wilson, borrowing from Melville, would call "the shock of recognition," except that the effort in this instance was to express the mind of a generation through the books that shaped it. Cowley took counsel with a number of the journal's friends, all liberal intellectuals—Morris Cohen, Felix Frankfurter, Kenneth Burke, Lewis Mumford, Robert Lynd, and others—all of whom thought it was "a swell idea" and volunteered their suggestions. Twelve books made up the final list. The editors paired each with an appropriate essayist. The list, for the most part, was unexceptionable. It included *The Education of Henry Adams,* Thorstein Veblen's *Theory of Business Enterprise,* Sigmund Freud's *Interpretation of Dreams,* V. I. Lenin's *The State and Revolution,* Oswald Spengler's *Decline of the West,* Charles A. Beard's *An Economic Interpretation of the Constitution,*

Franz Boas's *Mind of Primitive Man,* and the most recent of the books, Vernon L. Parrington's *Main Currents in American Thought.* A problem arose over which of John Dewey's many books to choose. In the end the philosopher asked to write the essay, C. E. Ayer, chose *Studies in Logical Theory* as the single most important work for the student of Dewey's mind and influence. The one shocker was the inclusion of William Graham Sumner's *Folkways,* with its social Darwinist perspective. The series completed, Cowley added a postscript in which he apologized for the omission—I didn't see why—of *Mein Kampf,* as well as any work treating the physical universe, perhaps Alfred N. Whitehead's *Science and the Modern World.* Cowley searched the essays for some single interpretive theme, finally, and quite arbitrarily, coming up with "The End of Reasoning Man."

In any attempt to identify "the books that changed my mind," I would carry over from the *New Republic* list *The Education of Henry Adams,* Veblen, though with another title, *The Theory of the Leisure Class,* and, particularly, Parrington's *Main Currents.* That work struck me at the most formative time of my education and left an indelible mark. A son of the Middle Border, Parrington was educated at Harvard, and he spent most of his career as an obscure professor of English at the University of Washington. In 1913, the year of Beard's *Economic Interpretation of the Constitution,* Parrington began to write a literary history of the United States in the same socioeconomic vein. The first two volumes, *The Colonial Mind* and *The Romantic Revolution,* appeared in 1927; the projected third volume, *The Beginnings of Critical Realism,* was left sadly incomplete by the author's death in 1929 but was published in fragmentary form the next year.

Following the broad road of political, economic, and intellectual development, rather than the formally belletristic, Parrington dealt with forces and ideas anterior to literary schools and movements and with materials that ramified into theology, science, and ethics. At the outset, he avowed his point of view, "liberal rather than conservative, Jeffersonian rather than Federalistic." These were the galvanizing abstractions of American political history, and he further defined the ideological conflict as "largely a struggle between the spirit of the Declaration of Independence and the spirit of the Constitution, the one primarily concerned with the rights of man, the other more practically concerned with the rights of property." Jefferson was the hero nonpareil. "To all who profess faith in the democratic ideal," wrote Parrington, "Jefferson is a perennial inspiration. A free soul, he loved freedom enough to deny it to none; an idealist, he believed that the welfare of the whole, and not the prosperity of any group, is the single end of government. He was our first great leader to erect a philosophy native to the economics and experience of America, as he was the first to break consciously with the past. His life was dedicated to the service of freedom."

In Parrington's conception American liberalism passed through three main stages. First was the stage of naturalization, which saw the disintegration of Old World tyrannies under the pressure of a free environment and the emergence of a revolutionary philosophy in harmony with native conditions and ideals. The crucial political conflict of this stage culminated in the struggle between Jefferson and Alexander Hamilton. This was the archetypal conflict of American politics. Every student had read Claude G. Bowers's exciting book *Jefferson and Hamilton* in 1925. It voted for Jefferson on every page. To it Parrington added his own conceptual slant. Although Jefferson was the victor as far as ballots and sentiments could decide the issue, Hamilton prevailed in the course of history. "Hamiltonian principles," Parrington wrote, "lie at the core of the problem that has proven so difficult of solution by modern liberalism." That self-interest is the mainspring of ambition, that power follows property and government exists for its protection, that the state should wield its scepter to extend the field of profitable operations and safeguard exploitation, that it should therefore be so constituted as to check popular rule and insure the ascendancy of the propertied class—these were the founding axioms of the Constitution, and Hamilton became its chief executor. He was, said Parrington, "the creative organizer of a political state answering the needs of a capitalistic order."

In the second volume of *Main Currents,* Parrington charted the fortunes of liberalism in three strategic cultural centers. In the South, the slaveholders' white-porticoed dream of a Greek democracy eclipsed the eighteenth-century vision of an agrarian democracy. All that remained of Jeffersonian principle was its state-rights constitutionalism deployed, moreover, not in defense of freedom but of the chattel slavery Jefferson had sought to put on the road to extinction. On the western frontier, where nature seemed its best guarantee,

Jeffersonianism fell victim to the acquisitive spirit—to what Veblen called "agrarian cupidity." The idea of freedom became the freedom to exploit, the idea of equality became equality in the pursuit of the main chance, the idea of progress an excuse for aggrandizement. The best expression of the liberal faith in the middle period came in New England, Parrington thought. Unfortunately, the social message of the Yankee writers and rebels was buried under abstruse metaphysics, and their numerous causes and experiments were, the author wrote, but "the last flowerings of the tree that was dying at its roots." The outraged conscience of New England moralists, mystics, and Utopians was ineffectual against the forces of industrial capitalism. And with the subsidence of the transcendental ferment, the New England mind slipped easily under "the reign of the genteel."

Critical realism—the theme of the unfinished third volume—was the name Parrington gave to the new method of liberalism forged in the agrarian revolt and the post-Darwinian science of the late nineteenth century. "Through it all runs increasingly a note of sobering realism," Parrington observed. "After a hundred years political romanticism was dying in America." Critical realism, although disillusioning, instructed liberals in the ways and the uses of power. This was the substantial result of that "great stock-taking adventure," the progressive movement, early in the new century. Beard's *Economic Interpretation of the Constitution* was the chief educator. But Beard did not stand alone. He had a precursor in J. Allen Smith, whose *The Spirit of American Government* appeared in 1907, and the skepticism of the populist revolt pervaded the movement. The point is developed in one of the fragments of the third volume, the brilliant essay entitled "A Chapter in American Liberalism." "Democratic aspiration," Parrington wrote, "had been thwarted hitherto by the uncontrolled play of the acquisitive instinct; the immediate problem was the control of that instinct in the common interest. Economics had controlled the political state to its narrow and selfish advantage; it was for the political state to resume its sovereignty and extend its control over economics." With this Parrington might have shaken hands with Herbert Croly, the founding editor of the *New Republic*.

But the promise of the new realism was not fulfilled, for, as Parrington wrote, "the war intervened and the green fields shriveled in an afternoon. With the cynicism that came with post-war days the democratic liberalism of 1917 was thrown away like an empty whiskey flask." From the war came the pessimistic science of psychology—"the moron emerged as a singular commentary on our American democracy"—and then the theories of Freud and John B. Watson. "If the mass . . . never rises above sex appeals and belly needs, surely it is poor stuff to try to work up into an excellent civilization." Sinclair Lewis's *Babbitt* was the representative man of the twenties, "the symbol of our common emptiness," the end product of middle-class values. Parrington, the elder liberal, who had been warmed in the afterglow of the Enlightenment, found himself with his liberal contemporaries in "the unhappy predicament of being treated as mourners at their own funerals." He concluded his "Chapter on American Liberalism" on a melancholy note: "It is a discouraging essay."

Main Currents in American Thought was, I suppose, the primary piece of intellectual furniture I brought to graduate school. From my studies I learned to take a more discriminating view of it. In the book's treatment of major American authors particularly, Parrington's essentially political approach was a blunt critical instrument. It might work for Jefferson or Webster or even Whitman, but it did not work for Emerson or Hawthorne or Poe or James. Parrington's stature was already in decline among scholars, and it has fallen further since, indeed to the point where he is seldom read or consulted except as a minor figure in the history of American letters. But for me, whatever his aesthetic deficiencies, Parrington opened a highway to that "usable past" which so many liberals had despaired of finding.

Born in New York in 1895, Lewis Mumford described himself as "a child of the city." From the brownstone home of his youth on the Upper West Side, he explored the city on foot from Central Park to the Brooklyn Bridge and much in between, making observant notes of the urban landscape and its architecture. As Thoreau could say he had traveled "a great deal in Concord," Mumford could say the same of himself in Walt Whitman's "Manahatta." It was, he added, "my university." He attended City College, with hopes of becoming a philosopher, and, after an enforced break caused by a tubercular condition, he attained his bachelor's degree in 1917. Along the way he discovered his true master, the aged Scotsman Patrick Geddes, who aspired to achieve a synthesis of evolutionary biology and sociology, and whose ideas about the growth of cities in Western history put Mumford on the track of his great theme. Always an idealist at war with the pragmatists of the day, Mumford's penchant would sometimes find passionate expression, as it did in 1940 in his *New Republic* article "The Corruption of Liberalism."

After a stint in the navy during the war, Mumford returned to New York and began a literary apprenticeship on the editorial desks of two metropolitan magazines, the fortnightly *Dial,* where he made the acquaintance of Thorstein Veblen, and the weekly *Freeman.* Here he started a lifelong friendship, even discipleship, with Van Wyck Brooks, the Harvard-educated literary critic whose manifesto, *America Comes of Age,* in 1915, became the rallying point of a group, the Literary Radicals, pledged to a renascence of American letters. Paul Rosenfeld, Waldo Frank, and Randolph Bourne, no longer living, were among the group. At Brooks's suggestion, Mumford wrote his first book, *A Story of Utopias,* a hop, skip, and a jump through Utopian writing from Plato to Edward Bellamy. It was followed in 1924 by *Sticks and Stones,* a study of late-nineteenth-century American architecture viewed as an index to civilization. The book, although slight, won high praise from Frank Lloyd Wright, the country's foremost architect; and Mumford, had he chosen, might have made his career in this field.

He also dabbled for a time in American literary history. *The Golden Day,* in 1926, skated charmingly over thin ice from the seventeenth to the twentieth century. The heart of the book was a seventy-two–page essay on "The Golden Day," wherein the authors Thoreau, Hawthorne, Melville, and Whitman revolved around their sun, Emerson. For Mumford, no less than for Brooks, Emerson was the key figure of that usable past they hoped to reclaim. Earlier radical critics, with H. L. Mencken in the lead, had found the literary past a wasteland. Now it was affirmed for its youthful anticipations. "We are the pioneers of the world," Melville had written, and Mumford had copied, "the advance guard, sent on through the wilderness of untried things, to break a new path in the New World. . . . In our youth is our strength; in our inexperience, our wisdom." *The Golden Day* was Mumford's first publishing success. As his biographer has written, it "set the seal on his reputation as a first-rate literary and philosophic mind." It inspired a rising generation of Americanists. F. O. Matthiessen, among the best of them, said the book was "a major event in my experience." He was the one, of course, who turned Mumford's sketch into a monumental work of scholarship, *American Renaissance,* in 1941.

Mumford's reputation rests much more securely, however, on the series of philosophical works treating the history of Western civilization to which he gave the overall title "The Renewal of Life." The title says a lot about Mumford's approach: history was never past for him, it was a luminous guide to a better future. The first two, and most influential, of these volumes, *Technics and Civilization* and *The Culture of Cities,* appeared in 1934 and 1938, respectively. Both were brilliantly illustrated. Mumford had a synthesizing mind and one thatsought capacious views.

When it came to selecting a title for the series *Books That Changed Our Minds,* he chose Oswald Spengler's *Decline of the West.* The German's cyclical theory of history, with its morbid prophecy of decline, found a rough parallel in Mumford's theory of stages, adapted from Geddes, though the American characteristically discerned signs of rebirth amid the decay. Each stage is defined largely by its principal source of industrial power. In the eotechnic it is wind, water, and wood; and life is organized in the village agricultural community. It is followed in the eighteenth century by the paleotechnic stage based upon coal and iron. Smoke-belching cities emerge; division of labor sets in; mechanization takes command. This is the era of Blake's "dark satanic mills." It is followed in the latter part of the nineteenth century by the neotechnic phase based upon power from electricity. Like Henry Adams, in his theory of history, Mumford postulated that with the acceleration of technological advance each stage succeeded another more and more rapidly. "The city under the influence of the capitalistic mythos concentrates upon bigness and power." Metropolis becomes Megalopolis, thence sinks into tyranny and decadence. But Mumford rescued the city and the machine in a new biotechnic era in which technology nurtures the culture of life. "In the biotechnic order the biological and social arts become dominant: agriculture, medicine, and education take precedence over engineering."

These books are full of unforgettable aperçus such as "The Monastery and the Clock." The clock, said Mumford, is the key machine of the industrial age, yet it originated, ironically, in the monasteries of the fourteenth century. By fixing and tolling the passage of time, the clock epitomized the transition from heavenly to worldly vocations. "In its relationship to determinable quantities of energy, to standardization, to automatic action, and finally . . . to accurate timing, the clock has been the foremost machine in modern technics." Another instance is London's Crystal Palace of 1851. It rose in Hyde Park at the height of the grimy paleotechnic stage, yet anticipated the neotechnic. "For the modern forms of masonry it substituted the relative lightness of the iron skeleton; for the solid masses and enclosures of the old-fashioned supporting walls, the new design substituted open space bounded by mere filaments of glass."

Culture of Cities was not only about cities; it was about regions. Mumford was a founding member of the Regional Planning Association of America. "The re-animation and re-building of regions, as deliberate works of collective art," Mumford wrote, "is the grand task of politics for the opening generation." As architecture was properly the servant of life, not of art or industry, as towns and cities were the service centers of communities, so were regions the best organizing principle for the government of larger areas. Mumford was profoundly influenced by Ebenezer Howard's landmark, turn-of-the-century reconfiguration of English towns and countryside in *Garden Cities of Tomorrow*. He cheered the achievements, such as they were, of the Resettlement Administration under the New Deal. And with his liberal friends, he saw in the Tennessee Valley Authority a model for reconstructing government on regionalist principles. He realized, however, that under the regime of private property and pecuniary economy, progress must be halting at best.

Mumford's mind was fundamentally apolitical. I found his goals admirable, but in his philosophy there was no social or economic or political dynamic working to advance them. They were castles in the air. There were elements of Marxism in his system. The emphasis he placed upon industrial technology was on speaking terms with Marxian historical materialism. But Marx and Engels postulated the class struggle as the force for revolutionary change of an exploitative economic system. And Marxism assumed that changing means of production determined the course of ideas and politics. In Mumford it was the other way around; the mind made the technology and the institutions. His philosophy, in short, existed in a Platonic void.

Mumford was an independent radical who earned his living with his pen. As a scholar he was self-made. He never seriously considered pursuing an academic career, though he taught briefly at a number of universities during his lifetime. In this he fit the pattern of the literary radical, as set by Brooks, but one represented as well in the lives of such intellectuals as Edmund Wilson and Alfred Kazin. Mumford's best work was done before he veered off course and wrote *Men Must Act* in 1939, albeit that was a true service. He completed "The Renewal of Life" with *The Condition of Man* and *The Conduct of Life* in 1944 and 1951, respectively. Here Mumford's prophetic, not to say apocalyptic, side overrode the historical and sociological. The turgidity of the prose obscured whatever message the books may have contained. Mumford's reformist zeal found expression in several postwar crusades: nuclear disarmament, the battle to save New York from grandiose megalopolitan development, and protest against the Vietnam War. When I met him in the fifties, he was a medium-sized man, handsome and thin, with a mustache, and his quiet reserve masked a fiery heart. Combining learning with passion, Mumford was a formidable figure on the intellectual landscape for some sixty years.

My reader's acquaintance with Max Lerner began with his first book, *It Is Later than You Think.* Mr. Purkaple, my high school teacher, must have recommended the book to me soon after its publication in November 1938. Lerner was a Russian-born immigrant child who grew up in the environs of New York and attended Yale University on a scholarship. He earned his Ph.D. at the Robert S. Brookings Graduate School of Economics and Government, forerunner of the Brookings Institution, in Washington. He wrote his dissertation on Thorstein Veblen, his intellectual idol; and Veblen was a favorite theme for many years. His professional career began as managing editor of the massive *Encyclopedia of the Social Sciences,* an indispensable scholarly resource for the next thirty or forty years. In the mid-thirties he was the young political editor of the *Nation.* Later, of course, he was prominently associated with the *New Republic.* In 1938, after an editorial quarrel led to his dismissal from the *Nation,* Lerner became professor of political science at Williams College in the Berkshires. He had taught before, at Harvard and Sarah Lawrence, but the retired life of the teacher and scholar never seemed to agree with him for long. He was fond of quoting Justice Holmes, another of his heroes, "as life is action and passion, it is required of a man that he should share the passion and action of his time at peril of being judged not to have lived."

For Lerner this meant the world of journalism. In 1943, as earlier noted, he became the chief editorial voice of *PM*. Writing to meet daily deadlines honed and challenged Lerner's broad-gauged mind. Later, when I had a teaching relationship with him, I was constantly astonished by his readiness to say something of interest about almost anything under the sun. He was a confessed movie addict and might have been a terrific film critic. Likewise, had he limited himself, he could have been a fine constitutional lawyer, historian, social planner, or half a dozen other things. At the *Encyclopedia*, he collaborated with a young colleague to write a long article—over eight thousand words—on literature and society. Lerner, like most Jewish intellectuals, was always most at home in New York. Returning there in 1943 after five years in Arcadia, he penned a tribute, "Hello Again, New York": "Hello again to the taxis, which have created a breed of man unparalleled in history—men who become practicing psychologists without studying Freud, and rule-of-thumb philosophers without reading Plato or Spinoza; in whom has been condensed all the turbulence of the city." Wherever and as long as *PM* was read, Lerner was an influence to reckon with. As a favorite student, now his biographer, Sanford Lakoff, has reminded us, John Gunther, in his bestselling *Inside U.S.A.*, referred to a patrician friend who remarked on the power of Minsk in American culture and politics. Why Minsk? the author asked. And he was answered: "Because Minsk is the birthplace of Max Lerner . . . Lerner runs *PM*. *PM* runs the American Labor Party. The American Labor Party runs New York City. New York City runs New York state. And New York state runs the nation."

In his foreword to *It Is Later than You Think*, Lerner called the book "an essay in the philosophy and tactic of democratic collectivism." And democratic collectivism, building upon the New Deal, was the new economic foundation necessary to the survival of liberalism. The old foundation was laissez-faire and the free market, the economy of bourgeois capitalism, which collapsed in the Great Depression. The core of liberalism remained what it was for Locke, Jefferson, Mill, and other worthies; "it is only the garments and the weapons that are changed, because the old ones are worn out." Yet the chameleon quality of the word *liberal* troubled Lerner, and he wrote, "I am far more a democrat than I am a liberal." This expressed a confidence in the will of the people and majority rule that transcended doctrinaire agendas, conservative or liberal. He disapproved of his English friend Laski's abandonment of liberalism as a mere facade of capitalist power, on the one hand, and Walter Lippmann's appropriation of the word in *The Good Society* (1937) as a baptismal confirmation of that regime, on the other hand.

Militant was a favorite adjective for Lerner, as it was for Mumford. The book bore the subtitle *The Need for a Militant Democracy*. The United States was "a crisis state," both because of the strivings required to put its own house in order and because fascism had to be defeated abroad. Its democracy must be tough-minded, in William James's sense; it must have the strength to will collectivization; it must have sufficient confidence in its own tolerance to root out fascists in its midst. Never a committed Marxist, Lerner never experienced the collapse of high radical hopes. In his book he made a syllabus of Marxism's errors: It underestimated the resiliency of capitalism. It overestimated the revolutionary character of the proletariate. It mistook the character and the aspirations of the middle class. The Marxians failed to understand nationalism, "the most powerful emotional force in modern history, and hand[ed] it over to the enemy." Their theory of human nature was archaic, and they erred in supposing a proletarian dictatorship, once imposed, could be readily lifted. After my own flirtation with Marxism, I could say amen to all this while still endorsing Lerner's conclusion: for all its faults and shortcomings, Marxism is the most illuminating body of social thought in our world.

What is perhaps most interesting about the book in retrospect is that, while it observes the Left in retreat, it also observes the seeds of renewal in "the rediscovery of the past." Lerner named this the most important development in the radical movement. Reversing Lincoln Steffens, Lerner might have said, "I have seen the past; and it works." Americans on the liberal-left were engaged in "a new Research Magnificent—the rediscovery of the nation and the sentiments that cluster around it." This new traditionalism on the part of intellectuals who had previously dismissed the national past had its naive, even dangerous, aspect. Lerner hoped it would not become an exercise in American exceptionalism, making us secessionists from world history, but instead would become a new amalgam of radicalism and nationalism in a "transnational fellowship."

Lerner was an engaging essayist. The form was really his *metier.* In 1939 and 1941 he published back-to-back collections: *Ideas are Weapons* and *Ideas for the Ice Age.* They ranged widely over many subjects but were most impressive in the field of American constitutional law. He had published the first of these pieces, "The Social Thought of Mr. Justice Brandeis," in the *Yale Law Journal* in 1931. It was followed by "The Supreme Court and American Capitalism," in the same place in 1933. To call these essays is perhaps a misnomer; they are, truly, monographs with all the earmarks of scholarship, yet touched with literary grace. The thesis of the latter, traced through successive periods, is that judicial review of the Constitution was "merely the *modus operandi* of business enterprise." The influence of Veblen was evident, even more so that of Beard's *Economic Interpretation.* But Lerner was no uncritical admirer of that work. "It was oversharp," he wrote, "by making the economic interpretation a theory of men's motives rather than of men's ideas."

The book of Lerner's that I treasure beyond any other is *The Mind and Faith of Justice Holmes.* I purchased it in the first edition in 1943. It is surely one of the most creative anthologies ever constructed, made of diverse and unpromising materials—judicial opinions in large part—and kept together by a thread of brilliant commentary. Lerner, the Jewish boy from Minsk, and Holmes, the Boston Brahmin, had nothing in common except an intellectual fascination with the law and with meaning. Lerner liked wrestling with the paradox of the justice's "austerity theory" of the judicial process, transcending personal predilection or notions of social policy, on one side, yet reasoning to conclusions that sustained his activist colleague Brandeis's opinions based upon sociological data, on the other. I do not know whether the two men—Lerner and Holmes—ever met and talked, but if they did, it must have been a rousing conversation.

S I X

Cold War

In 1946 the *New Republic*'s circulation was at an all-time high, 45,000, and young Michael Straight assumed the leadership of the weekly his parents had founded. Straight, according to Bruce Bliven, conceived of the *New Republic* as "a liberal *Times*" with a wide readership. This implied expanded coverage with more attention to hard news. Straight, in his own account of these years, said simply, "I wanted to liven it up." The magazine soon reflected the change. The addition of line drawings, wood engravings, and lithographs to the pages gave them a new look. The magazine's politics, and its newsstand price, remained the same. The editorial foursome of Bliven, George Soule, Straight, and Stark Young signed a "Statement of Faith" in April. Their position was defined as independent, nondogmatic "militant liberalism," and they paraphrased the famous oath of William Lloyd Garrison upon launching the *Liberator:* "We are in earnest. We will not equivocate. We will not excuse, and we will be heard." Important changes of staff occurred. Helen Fuller became the Washington reporter; Shirley O'Hara succeeded Manny Farber as film critic; Irwin Shaw soon replaced the veteran Young; and Soule, another veteran, slowly withdrew. The biggest loss, in my opinion, was Malcolm Cowley. He continued as a contributor, but he had no true successor in the literary department. New departments were added, including a UN column, a radio column, and a farm column.

However, a bigger change occurred at year's end. When Henry A. Wallace was forced to resign his post as secretary of commerce in a conflict with the president over foreign policy, Straight hastily invited the old New Dealer and global crusader to become editor. Straight thought that Wallace's name at the top of the masthead would boost circulation and realize his dream for the journal. Coincident with Wallace's arrival in December, the *New Republic* was made over. The size of the page—now printed in three columns rather than two—shrank, but the number of pages increased—the weekly was substantially fatter than before. The typography was changed, and color appeared on the cover. Bliven, the "editorial director," managed day-to-day operation of the magazine; but Wallace quickly placed his imprint upon it, and this would lead to difficulties. Bliven would later devote a chapter in his memoir to this period; he titled it "The Great Wallace Debacle." When he became a presidential candidate early in 1948, Wallace resigned the editorship, but, with Straight's approval, he continued to figure prominently in the pages of the *New Republic* as a columnist, which some thought compromised the magazine's independence.

The prosperity generated by the war survived in the peace yet brought its own problems and kept politics in turmoil. The *New Republic* feared the recurrence of the "normalcy" syndrome from the era after the First World War, and to a degree its fears were justified. Demobilization and reconversion proceeded at a breakneck pace. Because disposable income outran the supply of goods and services, inflation grew alarmingly. Yet price controls collapsed within two years, and little was done to meet crucial shortages. When attempts were made, remedial legislation was usually blocked, as with housing and the real estate lobby. Harry Truman, however, was no Warren G. Harding. The bespectacled little man in the blue serge suit, with a dry Missouri voice that lowered public oratory to new depths, failed to inspire, yet his plodding earnestness drew grudging respect. He stood in the shadow of Franklin D. Roosevelt, so the *New Republic* could never see him in a heroic light. Constantly measuring him, it conceded he had a liberal program, and it made allowance for a recalcitrant Congress that repeatedly humiliated him. When Truman fought back, as in his veto of "a fake price control bill," the magazine cheered him on. It was, the editors said, "the most statesmanlike action" of his presidency, to which T. R. B. added, "He said 'No' resolutely. He said 'No' with bells on it." Of course, the liberals' hope for adoption of "an American Beveridge Plan" went out the window, though some pieces of it were enacted in mangled form. A proposed full employment bill would have established a procedure for adjusting federal spending annually to ensure full employment for the nation's welfare. Although a defeat for the administration, said the *New Republic,* the watered-down bill passed by Congress was in its stated purpose of historic importance. The president was unfortunate in the men gathered around him, the editors felt. Harding had had his "Ohio Gang," Truman had his "Missouri Buddies," mediocrities every one, who did nothing for him and on occasion hurt him. Still, Soule wrote reflectively, "It Was Worse Last Time."

Eager to maintain the Roosevelt Coalition in the Democratic Party, the *New Republic* backed the aggressive campaign of organized labor (AF of L and CIO) to share in the new prosperity. Labor's aim was to retain the take-home pay of wartime after return to the normal forty-hour week. It sought as well to keep wages abreast of the rising cost of living. A wave of strikes swept the nation. The biggest were in the automobile and steel industries. Walter Reuther of the United Automobile Workers subscribed to the theory that higher wages were the key to prosperity. Early in 1946, 350,000 autoworkers struck General Motors for a 30 percent wage increase. When the union sought information on GM profits, management replied it was "none of the Union's damned business," reported Reuther in an article written for the *New Republic.* Soule, then writing to save the excess profits tax, had shown that the after-tax profits of all U.S. corporations had doubled in the years between 1939 and 1945. Moreover, he argued in a follow-up that "Profits Are Public Business." But Reuther was not satisfied to rest his case on fairness. "The fight of the General Motors workers is a fight to save truly free enterprise from death at the hands of its self-appointed champions." And he went on, "Labor is not fighting for a larger slice of the pie. Labor is fighting for a larger pie." Reuther finally settled for something less,

18½ cents an hour, which was in line with the recommendation of the government's fact-finding board; and this set the standard for wage increases in all American industry.

In the bituminous coal industry, John L. Lewis, "Old Eyebrows," tried to better the standard. The operators refused the demand, the miners walked out, and the government seized the mines. Lewis, "the feudal baron," as the *New Republic* called him, prevailed in this standoff; and then, in the fall, he tried to reopen the contract for a second-round increase. A strike was threatened; the government got an injunction, which Lewis defied; the federal judge fined the United Mine Workers exorbitantly; and the miners returned to the pits while the decision was appealed. In the end, the old baron prevailed again, and the miners got the best contract they had ever had. Meanwhile, a nationwide railroad stoppage threatened disaster to the economy. The president appealed to the strikers to return to work, and when that failed he went to Congress and requested emergency powers that, among other things, would provide for drafting strikers into the army. A bill for this purpose sailed through the House of Representatives on the same day. The *New Republic* was outraged. "Truman's Blunder," the lead editorial screamed. "The bill would take the United States a terrifyingly long step on the road to fascism." It was an unprecedented blow to organized labor. But the journal's editors screamed too soon. The railroad brotherhoods yielded to the president's demands; the workers returned, and the punitive bill was set aside.

Rapid growth of union membership, spurred by the war, continued afterward. "Big Labor," taking its place beside "Big Business" and "Big Government," became a force to reckon with. The one section of the country virtually untouched by the trend was the South. The CIO launched an aggressive organizing drive in the southern textile mills in 1946. Quite aside from the first aim of improving the lives of workers in grimy milltowns, the union organizers sought to exert political leverage upon reactionary southern Democrats. The *New Republic* watched this development with interest. Lawrence Lader's article "It's Still Done the Hardway," in mid-1947, was a first-hand report from Georgia's milltowns. Organizers' lives were in constant danger, and the collective bargaining rights of the National Labor Relations Act were openly flouted. Race, with all the terrors gathered round it, was a fearful deterrent. One organizer, Ernie Stowner, observed: "If we could only lick the race issue, we could really move ahead. The companies are playing whites against Negroes, Negroes against whites." There was, he thought, an education job to be done in the South before union organization could proceed very far.

Labor's worst setback during these years, the Taft-Hartley Act, came in the wake of the Republican sweep in the congressional election of 1946. As it had since 1940, the magazine published its roll-call vote analysis and handbook. It showed, most significantly, how the votes of southern Democrats, joined with the Republicans, swung the decision on important domestic issues. The editors urged readers to work with independent liberal groups:

National Citizens Political Action Committee, CIO-PAC, and Union for Democratic Action. The November result was even worse than feared, however. "We Were Licked!" the magazine headlined its election roundup. The number of Democrats fell from 241 to 187 in the House and to a minority of 45 in the Senate, where eleven of that number voted against the party over half the time. As bad as it was, the editors observed, the debacle was not a positive rejection of the New Deal. It was, rather, the outcome of apathy in the electorate. While a popular vote of 43 million had been reliably projected, only 35 million turned out. Political ineptitude by the Democratic Party was the culprit. The *New Republic* tagged it the third phase of the New Deal downturn, the first having come in 1938, and the second in 1942. Passage of the antilabor Taft-Hartley Act by the Eightieth Congress was a foregone conclusion. President Truman vetoed it in a message the journal called the most powerful state paper to come from his pen. The veto was promptly overridden, however, and the editors laid the blame on the president for failing to rally his party. After attacking labor, the main objectives of the ultraconservative Congress were to cut taxes and kick the communists.

The onset of the Cold War loomed large in this period. I think, in retrospect, that was the most devastating great event, barring the Holocaust, of my lifetime. It was more devastating than the Second World War for that was "the good war," and it was bravely, effectively, and expeditiously fought to a victorious conclusion. No sooner had it been won, however, than the two great allies, the United States and the Soviet Union, fumbled away the peace in a spiraling conflict with each other. Following the course of international events in my daily and weekly reading, including the *New Republic,* I found it difficult to understand what was happening and to apportion blame for it.

Perhaps, as has sometimes been argued, the first big mistake was made by the United States in the diplomacy surrounding control of the atom bomb, or, indeed, that the mistake began with President Truman's decision to drop the bomb in the first place, without warning, on a defenseless city, killing 100,000 people. After the peace and the birth of the United Nations, the administration took the position that the bomb was "a sacred trust" and so would not be shared or wholly submitted to international control. This, said the *New Republic,* made all our lofty sentiments and democratic pleadings sound hypocritical to peoples of the world. Others thought it foreboded "a new imperialism." How much better would it have been if, instead of exciting suspicion and fear, the United States had convened an international conference to deal openly with the subject. The Senate Committee on Atomic Energy, meanwhile, listened to the testimony of nuclear scientists on the destructiveness of the bomb and toyed with the scenario of forty million American fatalities in the next war. Reporting these hearings, the magazine focused on the testimony of Dr. Philip Morrison of Los Alamos. The bomb rendered war obsolete. The science and technology that made it could not for long remain the monopoly of one nation. The trick, he said, was through international control to turn nuclear power into an instrument of peace. "We have a chance to build a working peace on the novelty and terror of the atomic bomb." A year after the bomb was dropped, the American people got a wrenching human report on the weapon in John Hersey's *Hiroshima*. Because it first appeared in a single issue of the *New Yorker,* it was an event in publishing history as well. The shock of reading it remains with me after half a century. At this time, the United Nations debated the plan drafted by Bernard M. Baruch, the American representative to its Atomic Energy Commission, for establishment of an International Atomic Development Authority. Awesome in scope and aim, the plan placed all nuclear energy under international control. It barred production for war purposes and authorized inspection and punishment of violators undeterred by big-power veto in the Security Council. Baruch concluded the report with a paraphrase of the famous words of Abraham Lincoln: "We cannot escape history. . . . We shall nobly save, or meanly lose, the last best hope of earth." Unfortunately, the Soviet Union, which did not yet have the bomb, refused to accept suspension of the veto, and this doomed the effort. Distrustful of American intentions, and fearing American domination of the proposed international body, the Russians shared responsibility for sowing these dragon teeth.

The control of atomic energy had its domestic side as well. Here debate centered around the confirmation of David E. Lilienthal as chairman of the new Atomic Energy Commission. I greatly admired Lilienthal. So did the *New Republic*. His little book *TVA: Democracy on the March* (1944) was a thrilling case study of what democratic state planning could accomplish. In 1945 Bliven wrote an enthusiastic three-part series on the agency. The *New Republic* adopted Lilienthal's idea of government enterprise as a regulatory "yardstick" in natural monopolies like electric power. It called for public authorities similar to the Tennessee Valley Authority (TVA) to be used on the St. Lawrence, in the Central Valley of California, and on the Columbia River, in accordance with President Roosevelt's vision of "Seven Little TVAs." Lilienthal, for all his success at the TVA, or perhaps because of it, met vigorous opposition as the president's nominee to chair the Atomic Energy Commission. One old enemy, Sen. Kenneth McKeller of Tennessee, fought him tooth and nail; Robert A. Taft, of Ohio, the Senate majority leader and a leading presidential candidate, called him "a typical power-hungry bureaucrat" and accused him of being soft on communism. As the confirmation hearings dragged on, the *New Republic* made comparison to the protracted proceedings on Louis D. Brandeis's nomination to the Supreme Court in 1916. But Truman stuck by Lilienthal; he finally prevailed, and the AEC got off to a fair start.

The world was full of hot spots—Palestine, China, Indonesia—but the hottest was India. In March 1946 the British Labor government under Prime Minister Attlee offered India unconditional independence and self-government under any terms that would satisfy the major parties of Hindus and Muslims. Reporting from New Delhi, the old India hand H. N. Brailsford still held out hope for a compromise that would take the form of a confederation between India and Pakistan. This proved impossible, however, and horrendous violence and genocide occurred as the two communities went their separate ways. Partition, the last-gasp British solution for evacuation of its empire, took effect in 1947. Prime Minister Nehru, cabling the *New Republic* about it, described the ongoing famine, the communal violence, and the Indianization of the civil service. Borrowing a leaf from a country that had been new just a century and a half before, he announced a policy of nonentanglement in foreign affairs. A world of developing new nations, a Third World, broke upon my consciousness.

Harold Isaacs, an American foreign correspondent in the Far East, published a continentwide interim report, *No Peace For Asia,* in 1947. Reviewing it in the *New Republic,* Richard Watts, Jr., called it "an extremely gloomy book." And so it was. There was no peace in Asia, Isaacs maintained, because the Second World War settled nothing except the defeat of Japanese conquest. Korea, halved at the 38th parallel, was "a test-tube showing of the new era." Having been there aboard the USS *Parle,* I could endorse his observation: "The Americans had approached Korea in the most abysmal ignorance of the country."

China remained a disaster area, of course. Isaacs's portrait of Generalissimo Chiang Kai-shek was grimly disturbing. The myth built up around him in the United States, he wrote, "is one of the remarkable creations of our time." The *New Republic* agreed. With my poor undergraduate knowledge of Chinese history, I had tried to fathom the civil war occurring under cover of the greater war in China. I depended mainly on the reports of foreign correspondents, beginning with Vincent Sheean and followed by Anna Louise Strong, Edgar Snow, Agnes Smedley, and others. Cowley's review of Smedley's *Battle*

Hymn of China in 1943 introduced me to this utterly original American woman. She had gone to visit the Communist guerrillas in Yenan in 1938 and stayed for five years. She reported all the bloody disasters in the dual war, but she also told of how the people in the North, under the government of Mao Tse-tung and Chou En-lai, were learning to read, to sing, and to fight. She took a dim view of old China hands with their "treaty-fort mentality." They, in turn, smeared her as a Soviet spy. Some months after peace with Japan, the president sent Gen. George C. Marshall to arrange a truce between the warring Kuomintang, backed by the United States, and the Communists in the North. A truce of sorts was arranged, but Marshall returned home with a message of defeat. He had no confidence in Chiang's corrupt, repressive, and reactionary regime. The administration, nevertheless, continued assistance to Chiang. The balance in the civil war, meanwhile, swung decisively to the Communists. In December 1946, Theodore H. White, during a brief association with the journal, wrote the pessimistic "Lost: American Policy in China." He blamed the false policy on irrational fears of communism and the erroneous idea of China as a counterweight to the Soviet Union. The following year the editors estimated the United States had spent four billion dollars on aid to China and had thereby only put off the day of eventual Communist victory.

On March 5, 1946, at little Westminster College in Missouri, before an audience that included President Truman, Winston Churchill delivered an address that is sometimes taken as the signature announcement of the

Cold War between the West and the Soviet Union. "From Stettin in the Baltic to Trieste in the Adriatic," Churchill gravely intoned, "an iron curtain has descended across the Continent." He went on to say that though the Soviet Union might not desire war, it desired the fruits of war by the indefinite expansion of Communist power and doctrine. The *New Republic* passed off the address as another instance of Churchill's anti-Communist mania. Its eyes were trained on events in Europe. The previous fall Bliven had gone to Britain to report on the new Labor government and the progress of the nationalization of industry. The National Health Service was particularly interesting because of the president's recent message to Congress endorsing, in essence, the Wagner-Murray-Dingell Bill, which held the promise of lifting from the United States the ignominy of trailing the world in the use of government to serve the health needs of its citizens. The magazine printed approvingly an article called "The New Communism" from the *London Tribune,* the organ of Labor's left wing, led by Aneurin Bevan, Michael Foot, and Jennie Lee. Observing the strength of Communist Parties everywhere on the continent except in Holland, Greece, neutral Sweden and Switzerland, and fascist Spain and Portugal, the article attributed this to the dissolution of the Comintern and a more practical, less dogmatic, brand of communism. The Popular Front, it seemed, was alive and well. Sympathies of this kind led the anti-Stalinist *Partisan Review* to attack the *New Republic* as "The 'Liberal' Fifth Column." Six months later Straight visited England and found a bad case of jitters about the state of the world. He quoted a London banker: "I and my friends believe that this is 1936. If the Russians are not stopped now there will be war." This seemed to confirm Churchill; indeed, it repeated his prophetic warnings against Nazi Germany.

Henry Wallace entertained a more hopeful view. It was compounded of faith in the peoples of the world, in democracy, in welfare economics, and applied science, and of naivete about Soviet communism. Wallace, it may be recalled, had nearly been President Roosevelt's successor in the White House. This was the role most liberals had cast for him. Arthur M. Schlesinger, Jr., writing in a special memorial issue on Roosevelt a year after he died, compared Wallace to Thomas Jefferson, the legendary father of democracy, and said that the torch of the New Deal should have passed to him rather than, pathetically, to Truman. On September 12, six months after Churchill's speech, Wallace addressed a peace rally at Madison Square Garden. It was, as the *New Republic* said, "a desperate effort to halt the drift to war," and the editors endorsed Wallace's call for a real peace treaty between the U.S. and the USSR. The speech, which Wallace thought Truman had approved in advance, led directly to his dismissal from the cabinet. An editorial titled "After the Wallace Dismissal" called upon all progressives to enlist under the banner of the new Peace Party. The last New Dealer had left the administration, and Russia would understand that the last great advocate of the third way in foreign affairs had left the scene. The magazine promptly published in pamphlet form Wallace's confidential memorandum to Truman that formed the substance of his speech. Wallace himself, after accepting appointment as editor of the *New Republic,* embarked on a coast-to-coast speaking tour to advance his agenda.

At the time, certainly, I was entirely sympathetic with Wallace and might have joined the 6,700 readers who wrote letters applauding him on his stand. Coincidentally the *New Republic* carried an interesting dialogue, "The Liberals and Russia," between the columnists Joseph and Stewart Alsop, on one side, and Max Lerner on the other. It began arrestingly with the former asserting, "The Liberal movement is now engaged in sowing the seeds of its own destruction." Liberals were avoiding the overwhelming political reality of the time: the Soviet challenge to the West. By doing so they risked themselves and provoked homegrown fascism. Lerner replied to the Alsops that "like an iceberg, nine-tenths of their argument lies beneath the surface." And most of it was aimed at Wallace. "An American foreign policy that is guided by fear of Russian power must in the end—whatever its other pretensions—be guided by nothing else." So, forget about justice to the Spanish Republicans, justice for the Jews in Palestine, peace in China. Of course, he was for slapping the Russians down when they deserved it. However, Lerner went on, "So far from being realism, it is utmost political naivete to believe that out of the clash of two great fear-obsessed powers peace will somehow be born." The enemy of America, he concluded, "is not Russia but the paralysis of will which, faced by an impending clash of two power systems, thinks not how to avert it, but how to consolidate all forces behind it." Both sides in the debate filed rejoinders a month later. Why on earth, asked the Alsops, shouldn't we be obsessed with Russia? Lerner, reaching for psychological wisdom, replied, "because such an obsession is bound to shatter the peace, not cement it," adding that, as in individuals, psychosis would lead not to health but to breakdown. He called for a third, left-of-center way, between the "good guys" (the Americans) and the "sons-of-bitches," as the Alsops would have it. Needless to say, I agreed with Lerner.

A year after Churchill's "iron curtain" speech, President Truman raised the stakes in the Cold War dramatically when he went before Congress to proclaim what came to be known as the Truman Doctrine. Britain was pulling out of Greece; responding to pleas from the royalist government in Athens, Truman proposed the United States fill the vacuum with large-scale economic and military aid to resist communist subversion. Turkey was thrown into the bargain, for no discernible reason other than "the smell of oil" in her part of the world. Furthermore, the rationale of the proposal was global. "I believe," said the president, "that it must [be] the policy of the United States to support free peoples who are resisting attempted subjugation." In a world divided between free and oppressed nations, no one should doubt where the United States stood. And so the president made an open-ended commitment without regard to the reach of American resources, as Walter Lippman, among others, pointed out. In May Congress passed an initial $400 million aid package for Greece and Turkey. The *New Republic* vigorously disapproved. It had repeatedly taken the view that the Greek government was in the hands of right-wing monarchists who lacked popular support, and the alleged communist threat was a smokescreen. Constantine Poulas, the Overseas New Agency's correspondent, reported that the government was responsible for economic failures and was leveraging American anti-Soviet fears to subsidize its murderous campaign against the leftist democratic opposition. Wallace immediately took to the air to answer Truman with a speech Straight later claimed to have written. Without denying Greece's economic troubles, Wallace said they should be addressed by the United Nations and other international agencies, such as the International Bank. He said the same thing in the *New Republic:* The UN must mend the Greek economy and Greek political machinery. Unilateral intervention by the United States would simply exacerbate tensions with the Soviet Union. The magazine went on to publish the report of the UN's Food and Agricultural Organization on its earlier mission to Greece, which left the impression the problems were on their way to solution when Truman followed Churchill in tying Greece to the Cold War kite. The *New Republic* spread over two pages a celebrated David Low cartoon. It showed Secretary of State Marshall, who had been pursuing diplomacy in Europe, stepping into a conference room occupied by his Russian counterpart, V. M. Molotov, and others, garbed as a Greek peasant with a fez.

This "Turning Point in History," as T. R. B. labeled it, occurred against the background of a rising Red scare in the United States. The veteran liberal George Soule, reviewing James Burnham's latest book, *The Struggle for the World,* described it as a hysterical philippic against the Soviet Union, then observed, "Obsessive anti-communism is, in the long run, the most potent Communist agent in the United States." (Imagining the reactionary Burnham as a communist agent took some doing!) The drawn-out Senate hearing on Lilienethal's nomination to head the Atomic Energy Commission had proceeded on the theory that he was soft on Communism. The House Un-American Activities Committee had found a fertile new ground to conquer in Hollywood. The Truman administration picked up these cues. Only ten days after the Greek-aid proposal, the president issued the loyalty order for investigation and removal of "disloyal" federal employees. In his editorial, "A Bad Case of Fever," Wallace compared this new "witch hunt" to the Alien and Sedition Laws of 1798, a subject explicated by Saul Padover in "The Wave of the Past." Wallace, as if to show that his political naivete was not limited to the Soviet Union, trusted that the Supreme Court would declare Truman's executive order unconstitutional. Upon all this, of course, the Russians looked with some dismay. A contributor to the *New Republic* on the arts in Moscow told of a sure-fire dramatic hit still in rehearsal. The play, "The Russian Question" by Konstantine Simonov, was about an American journalist sent to Moscow with a large advance to write a book demonstrating that Russia wanted war with United States. Alas, he could find no evidence to support this; he lost the advance, his job, his wife, everything.

Meanwhile, George Kennan, the scholar-diplomat at the head of the newly established policy planning staff of the State Department, matured its program for the revival of the war-devastated economies of Western Europe. In June 1947, this was set forth publicly by the secretary of state at the Harvard commencement and became known as the Marshall Plan. I was privileged to be in the audience. Marshall was careful to keep this plan of economic aid separate from the Truman Doctrine. "Our policy is directed not against any country or doctrine," the secretary declared, "but against hunger, poverty, desperation, and chaos." Unfortunately, the Soviet Union, although invited to participate, declined. Some observers suggested that the plan was, in fact, a "corrective" of the hastily proclaimed Truman Doctrine: a change of direction from ideological combat to straightforward economic assistance. Wallace and the *New Republic* at first viewed the Marshall Plan as a backhanded endorsement of their criticism of the Truman Doctrine. European observers reacted positively. David Schoenbrun cabled from Paris, "The Marshall Plan captured Europe's imagination like nothing I have ever seen." Even socialists on the Left were for it. It was, he said, "a tremendous diplomatic victory" for the United States. The Soviet Union, however, opposed the aid plan with vigor. In September there appeared a celebrated article, "The Sources of Soviet Conduct," by the mysterious Mr. X (soon identified as Kennan) in the prestigious journal *Foreign Affairs*. It advocated the "containment" of communism as the first principle of American foreign policy. This threw Wallace back on his heels, causing him to question once again the motivation and the thrust of the Truman administration's foreign policy.

During these years the *New Republic*'s columns reflected increasing national attention to civil rights questions, though no breakthroughs were recorded, and the hysteria over loyalty was a serious setback. As one who looked to a career in higher education, I took a keen interest in academic questions. Here the debate on curricular methods and goals tended to be polarized between the University of Chicago, where Robert M. Hutchins and Mortimer Adler reigned, and Harvard, then under the leadership of the scientist-educator James B. Conant. I considered the former, with its "great books" emphasis, medieval and found my prejudices confirmed in Sidney Hook's *Education for Modern Man* in 1946. Earlier I had read his mighty assault "The New Failure of Nerve" in *Partisan Review.* It was a moment of truth in my education. Fortunately, I was able to recognize it when I saw it. The Harvard approach was laid out, more or less, in *General Education in a Free Society.* F. O. Matthiessen reviewed the report in the *New Republic* under the title "Harvard Wants to Join America." Although it stressed the importance of a common core of knowledge, it was quite open and empirical in matters of curriculum.

Just as the year ended the cover was blown on one of the dirty secrets of American higher education: the quotas against Jews in leading eastern institutions. The practice was acknowledged by Ernest Hopkins, president of Dartmouth. Curiously, he seemed to think the quotas benefited Jews by keeping a lid on anti-Semitism, sure to worsen if more Jews got Ivy League degrees. The quotas would later be amply documented, reported upon, and denounced. Bliven, deeply interested, wrote a multipart series called "U.S. Anti-Semitism Today," which examined the topic from many angles, among them job discrimination, social clubs, and hate-mongering organizations. The founding of Brandeis University in 1948 owed something to the fact stated by Rabbi Stephen S. Wise, cited by Bliven: "The only occupation open to a Jew without resistance is the rabbinical profession." Carey McWilliams's *A Mask for Privilege* was a hard-hitting report on anti-Semitism in America. Being of a pro-Semitic nature, I applauded anything of this kind. The *New Republic* was also attentive to problems of Jewish refugees and survivors of the Holocaust and to the establishment of the new state of Israel. Among the few good works credited to President Truman was his lowering of barriers to the entry of Jews into the United States and, by pressure on Prime Minister Attlee, in Palestine, together with his instantaneous recognition of the new state of Israel in 1948.

The magazine also had praised Truman's civil rights message to Congress in the same year. Based upon the report of the president's own commission, the message urged passage of an antilynching bill, enactment of a permanent Fair Employment Practices Commission, and a standing Commission on Civil Rights. Helen Fuller, the Washington correspondent, called the report "a revolutionary document." Of course, it split the Democratic Party along its sectional seams and faced obstruction by the "Republocrats," a coinage that never made it against the favored "Dixiecrats." The Old South remained defiant. Demagogic governors like Herman Talmadge of Georgia ingeniously evaded the laws designed to prevent "lily white" primaries, and backed by a resurgent Ku Klux Klan, they terrorized Negroes who might be registered and dared to vote. No right was more important to southern Negroes, as Henry Lee Moon pointed out before the

1948 election, than the right to vote, as for the first time the Negroes had enough strength to contest the outcome in ten southern states. Most northern states had banned racial segregation in transportation, but it remained the rule in the South until after the famous decision in *Brown v. Board of Education* (1954). The government-sponsored tour of the Freedom Train, with its exhibit of treasured documents, awakened public interest in democratic ideals and also raised the question whether black and white would be allowed to visit it together south of the Potomac. The train drew huge crowds wherever it went. There was something about seeing the gift of freedom in tangible form. Forty-four-year-old Langston Hughes wrote a poem to celebrate, wryly, the Freedom Train.

> Lord, I been awaiten' for the Freedom Train!
> Down South in Dixie the only train I sees
> Got a Jim Crow car set aside for me.
> I hope there ain't no Jim Crow on the Freedom Train,
> No back entrance to the Freedom Train,
> No signs FOR COLORED on the Freedom Train,
> No WHITE FOLKS ONLY on the Freedom Train.
>   I'm gonna check up on this
>   Freedom Train.

My revisit to the *New Republic* after half a century confirms my impression that, despite expanded coverage after the war in the arts and letters and in science, it was less stimulating than in prior years. More was less. Malcolm Cowley, as earlier noted, never found a successor in literature. He scored a great success with his *Portable Faulkner* in 1946, with its imaginative creation of the saga of Yoknapatawpha County, the author's "mythical kingdom," as Robert Penn Warren named it, thereby making the author's work more intelligible to readers than it had been before. And he went on to write critical studies of classic American authors, including Nathaniel Hawthorne, Frank Norris, and Theodore Dreiser, some of them first published in the *New Republic*. In a review of one of Van Wyck Brooks's volumes in a series called "Makers and Finders," Cowley wrote a fine appreciation of that work. "Brooks is the first author in any language to make a [literary] tradition real and almost palpable by presenting it as a rich texture of meetings, readings, and ideas passed from one writer to another." With the rise of the New Critics, as Cowley recognized, he was falling out of fashion. After all, Brooks wrote above the text, never in it or from it.

An occasional book review in the magazine rose above the ordinary and alerted me to a book too important to be missed. This was true, for instance, of the six-page review of Alfred C. Kinsey's blockbuster *Sexual Behavior in the Human Male*. After a careful survey of the findings, the author, James R. Newman, lauded the work as "a triumph of sanity" and said it "laid the cornerstone of a great edifice in what until now was a wasteland." I later formed some acquaintance with the book and found, as did other readers, I suspect, a lot too strange to be believed. Indeed, my impression was summed up by the magazine's Paris correspondent: "The results of Kinsey's researches are rather astounding. If laws pertaining to sexual behavior were scrupulously enforced in the United States and all misdeeds punished, only five percent of American citizens would remain at liberty and the remaining 95 percent would be in jail." Arnold Toynbee was taken up as a prophet of doom in the Cold War. A clever abridgment of *The Study of History* made his ponderous work accessible, even popular, for the first time. I recall R. H. Crossman's review, reprinted from the *New Statesman,* "The Mythic World of Arnold Toynbee," saying that he had a medieval cast of mind and identified civilization with mystical religion. A year hence Crossman reviewed Toynbee's latest book, *Civilization on Trial,* wherein the author seemed to be fetching for a philosophy of history capable of challenging Marxism and beating the Russians.

Just as there was no adequate replacement for Cowley, so there was none for Stark Young in the drama department, though a succession of reviewers that included Harold Clurman tried to fill the void. The *New Republic* found itself the butt of the joke at the heart of Garson Kanin's play *Born Yesterday* in 1946. Judy Holliday starred as the dumb blonde (Billy Dawn) whose rich junkman-husband hires a rookie reporter on the magazine to make her more "couth." She protests, "But I'm not a dumb broad. I even read the *New Republic.*" The reporter asks if she has read an article in the current issue. Sure, she answers with her toothpaste smile, every word of it, twice, but she didn't understand any of it.

Undoubtedly, the premier drama to hit Broadway in the immediate postwar years was Tennessee Williams's *A Streetcar Named Desire.* It was a masterpiece, Irwin Shaw wrote in his review. The play also marked the arrival of the young American actor Marlon Brando, who "seems always on the verge of tearing down the proscenium with his bare hands." The best achievement in the dance was Martha Graham's *Appalachian Spring* with the music of Aaron Copland. From the moment I first saw it, heard it, it seemed to me the quintessentially American artistic creation. Cecil Smith, in a sensitive appreciation, wrote, "With Martha Graham the Puritan conscience has taken possession of the dance, giving that traditionally hedonistic form a moral fervor it has seldom known in modern times." (My mentor, Perry Miller, must have loved that.) The big news in motion pictures came not from Hollywood but from abroad. Roberto Rossellini's groundbreaking films *Open City* and *Paisan* were international sensations. English films, many of them from the J. Arthur Rank Studio, a number of them directed by David Lean, found an American audience for the first time. In Boston's Back Bay, the Exeter Theater, which doubled as a Unitarian church on Sundays, was the venue for English imports, and every other Saturday night, it seemed, my wife and I would be in the balcony watching films like *I Know Where I'm Going,* with Wendy Hiller, Lean's *Brief Encounter* or *Great Expectations,* and Alec Guiness comedies like *The Lavender Hill Mob.* The war, which had introduced us to pizza and revolutionized our eating habits, also internationalized our taste in the arts.

If one had ventured to the *New Republic*'s office on Madison Avenue and East Forty-ninth Street looking for the editor, Henry A. Wallace, one would seldom have found him. (In the spring of 1948 one might have had to cross a picket line manned by placard-carrying Wobblies protesting an offensive remark in Wallace Stegner's essay on their legendary hero Joe Hill.) The editor might have been at his 118–acre farm, "Farvue," fifty miles north of the city, where he raised chickens and otherwise engaged his agricultural vocation. Or he might have been traveling and speech-making at home or abroad.

The speeches, together with Wallace's weekly column in the *New Republic,* chart the course of his crusading presidential candidacy of a renascent Progressive Party. Near the end of December 1946, two weeks after he assumed the editorship of the magazine, Wallace attended the meeting of the Progressive Citizens of America (PCA), in Washington, and established his leadership of the organization. One week later, Americans for Democratic Action (ADA), backed by Eleanor Roosevelt, was born of a merger of two independent liberal voting groups. The *New Republic* deplored the division between the PCA and the ADA. It was as if the liberals had "moved into opposing trenches." Wallace himself, noting that the liberal movement was weaker than at any time since President Harding, addressed the issue in "The Enemy is Not Each Other" and called for a reconciliation. People wrote to him, "How does it happen that Henry Wallace and Mrs. Roosevelt are in opposing camps?" There was, however, a crucial ideological conflict between the two groups. The ADA rejected communists and their sympathizers, as did most trade unions, while the PCA sought to revive the Popular Front strategy of the thirties. Neither organization pledged support to Truman and his administration. But the ADA subscribed to the Truman Doctrine and the containment of communism. Wallace steadfastly refused to see the Soviet Union as an enemy. And if it acted aggressively abroad, it was only because it was provoked by reactionary American policies. After adoption of the Greek-Turkish aid package, Wallace observed, "every reactionary government and every strutting dictator will be able to hoist the anti-Communist skull and bones, and demand the American people rush to his aid." In the light of American policy toward such dictators as Francisco Franco, Chiang Kai-shek, and Argentina's Juan Perón, who could deny the truth of that? I certainly could not. Wallace's stance was non-communist rather than pro- or anti-communist. It was the same whether he was denouncing Red-baiting at home or abroad. "If I fail to cry out that I am anti-Communist, it is not because I am friendly to Communism, but because at this time of growing intolerance I refuse to join even the outer circle of that band of men who stir the steaming cauldron of hate and fear."

Wallace was not a good platform speaker, yet people flocked to hear him. In Chicago, 22,000 reportedly filled a stadium, and another 10,000 listened to loudspeakers outside. Often Paul Robeson was on hand hymning "Ol' Man River." At the invitation of the *New Statesman,* Wallace had earlier traveled to England for a round of speechmaking inaugurated by a BBC radio address on Sunday evening. "Wallace Shook 'Em," the Labor MP Michael Foot wrote from London, grateful to the American for clarifying the great issues between Western anti-communist imperialism and global democracy. David Low's cartoon, reprinted in the *New Republic,* showed a disheveled Wallace holding in one hand a box of hatching eggs and shading his searching eyes with the other as he says, "I am looking for the progressive forces that believe in world unity in behalf of peace." Off in a dark corner a man trapped under a collapsing "Great Wall of Europe" answers, "Here I am, Henry!" As he toured other European countries, Wallace was criticized at home for subverting American foreign policy. Sen. Arthur M. Vandenberg, Republican chairman of the Foreign Affairs Committee, called him an "itinerant saboteur"; others advocated revoking his passport and invoking the notorious Logan Act of 1798 against him. At home in July, Wallace was formally nominated for the presidency by the Progressive Party. He recognized the incompatibility between his candidacy and his editorship, and when asked to resign he immediately complied. Straight, Bliven, and company drew a sigh of relief, and although the magazine kept its pages open to Wallace, it pointedly did not support his campaign for the presidency.

Looking back, as I try to reconstruct my own thoughts and feelings about Wallace and his ill-starred crusade, two or three things seem clear. First, I admired Wallace as a statesman, yet could never feel any excitement about him. His best work had been done as Roosevelt's secretary of agriculture, where he had combined science, planning, and vision to improve agricultural production and to conceive the idea of an Ever Normal Granary worldwide. He was hard to figure out. For all his science, he was also a fuzzy-minded mystic. Second, I liked and generally approved of Wallace's ideas in foreign affairs, yet increasingly felt he was naive or unrealistic about Soviet intentions. What Lewis Feuer in the *New Republic* named "socialist imperialism" was incomprehensible in Marxian terms, and left-liberals like myself, like Wallace, were slow to recognize it. I, too, was non-communist with-out being anti-communist. That stance became increasingly difficult in 1948, however, after the Soviet coup and Jan Masaryk's suicide in Czechoslovakia and the Soviet blockade of Berlin, necessitating the massive Berlin air-lift. Third, I was puzzled by what Wallace hoped to accomplish by his candidacy. I dismissed any idea that he was a stalking-horse for the communists. I inclined to credit his own statement of purpose, "Stand Up and Be Counted." He had come to represent, he said, "the hope of world democracy" and felt the call to lead his country toward that ideal. The flip side of this was that his third-party candidacy would likely split the liberal vote and lead to President Truman's defeat by Republican challenger Thomas E. Dewey, in whom I had no confidence at all.

Truman was nominated at the Democratic Convention in Philadelphia in July. The *New Republic* viewed the nomination with gloom and foreboding. "Where is the Bryan of 1948 who can rescue the party from Wall Street domination?" it groaned. Three years after Roosevelt's death, his legacy had been exhausted by the Truman administration. "The challenge for the Democrats is to find a new progressive leader-ship or perish. . . . Today the liberal movement is without ideas. It is ignorant of its methods and uncertain of its ends. It is divided against itself, and so lacking in vision and guts that often its tune is called by the most reactionary groups on the extreme Right or extreme Left." Truman's chances of victory were rated just above zero, but the party had no viable alternative. He was expected to lose votes on the Left to Wallace, whose strength was put at 11 percent of the electorate in the spring, and on the Right to Strom Thurmond, the Dixiecrat candidate who vied for the electoral votes of five Deep South states. The highlight of the convention for me and many others was the rousing speech of Hubert Humphrey, the young mayor of Minneapolis, calling for adoption of a civil rights resolution— "a new emancipation proclamation"—in the face of the Dixiecrat revolt. "To those who say that this civil rights program is an infringement of states rights," Humphrey declared, "the time has arrived in America for the Democratic Party to get out of the shadow of states rights and walk forthrightly into the sunshine of human rights." Knowing the part these entangled concepts—state rights and human rights—had played in Jeffersonian politics, I felt at once that Humphrey's pronouncement, with the adoption of the resolution, marked a turning point in our history. After that the president's "scrappy" acceptance speech gave the party something to cheer about, even redeemed the convention in the eyes of the *New Republic*'s reporters. Truman denounced the "do-nothing" Eightieth Congress and vowed to call it into special session to enact needed legislation. Reports of the party's death had been exaggerated, Fuller wrote. The South had been scorned for the first time; a new era opened.

It was still, barely, the pretelevision era, and the campaign followed the usual course. President Truman's "whistle-stop" tour across the country attracted attention and galvanized the Democratic electorate. Portrayed as "a homespun country boy," he was, T. R. B. wrote, a David come to slay "the cold-blooded city slicker." Even so, his ultimate victory at the polls surprised nearly everyone but himself. Wallace, the Progressive candidate, won but a meager 2 percent of the popular vote, trailing the Dixie-crat Thurmond. Wallace had been blackened by the media and hopelessly discredited by what would soon be called McCarthyism. And so he retired to his farm on Long Island to raise chickens. In retrospect, he conceded he had been misled by the Soviet Union and deceived by the communists in his entourage. He made a clean break with them on the issue of Korea in 1950.

The *New Republic* went on, of course, but I, a decade-long reader, drifted away in the wake of "The Great Wallace Debacle." This may have had more to do with events in my own life than with a critical judgment of the magazine. But in the process of reinventing the *New Republic* and boosting its circulation, Michael Straight and company had made the magazine less interesting, less intellectually friendly, than it used to be. It had played an important role in my education, but the time had come to move on. Disillusionment with Henry Wallace was inseparable from my disillusionment with the magazine. In retrospect, I should have listened to Max Lerner's prediction in February after Wallace decided to run for president. "It will be a futile gesture," Lerner wrote, "with the main organizational strength provided by the Communists, whose prize victim and trophy Wallace has become. And the movement he leads will go down in history as a valiant but mistaken fringe-movement, instead of part of the central current of liberalism." That accorded exactly with my final judgment. Straight, meanwhile, labored manfully, as he later wrote, to salvage what he could of "the ruins of our publishing venture."

Brandeis

By June 1949 the progress on my doctoral dissertation was such that I thought to complete it and
take my degree on schedule one year hence and at the
same time acquire some needed teaching experience
part-time. Thus far my only classroom experience had
been as a teaching fellow in a course treating major
interpretations of American thought and institutions—
the work of Alexis de Tocqueville, James Bryce, Henry
Adams, Harold Laski, and others—taught by Professor
John Gaus of Harvard's government department. At first,
my search met with disappointment. Then one day it
occurred to me to try the brand-new university, Brandeis,
in nearby Waltham. Opened in 1948, Brandeis was set to
begin its second year with a second class of students. I
knew little about it except that it was new and in some
sense Jewish. My inquiry led to an appointment with
David Berkowitz, one of the faculty, who was performing
the duties of an academic dean or provost. After getting
acquainted, he told me that Max Lerner would be joining
the faculty in September as a commuter from New York
and that an assistant was wanted for the two courses he

would introduce, one on contemporary American civilization, the other an introduction to politics. The former would be required of all sophomores, approximately one hundred students, and the assistant would be responsible for holding discussion sections in the third hour of each week, grading papers, counseling students, and aiding the professor in other small ways.

My eyes lit up at the mention of Lerner. I had, after all, followed his career since he left Williams and joined *PM.* When *PM* folded, he went to the *New York Post,* and I saw his syndicated column on occasion. I was surprised to learn that he was making a return visit to the academy but excited by the prospect of association with him. Berkowitz asked me to go to New York for an interview with Lerner, who was vacationing at Southampton with his family. In that relaxed setting we hit it off beautifully. He explained that the big required course was based upon a book he had in hand. The book, *America as a Civilization,* ran to one thousand pages when it was finally published in 1957. Whatever else might be said of that work, it takes honorable place as the last major effort of a single author to interpret American life, thought, and institutions in comprehensive fashion, and so marks the end of a long tradition.

I got the job and was very happy in my association with Lerner and with Brandeis. My initial appointment was followed, in 1950, upon award of the Ph.D., with an assistant professorship. As one of the rare gentiles on the faculty, I must have attracted some notice. (We in this little tribe laughingly called ourselves "the early Christian martyrs.") The founding president, Abram L.

Sachar, in his memoir, *A Host at Last,* calls me "a young Kansan," by way of Harvard, and "the first major appointment in American history." He goes on to characterize me thus: "Peterson was a low-keyed, deliberate, circumspect, laconic personality, and he may have been bewildered by the intense, uninhibited types of student and faculty colleagues with which he had to deal." Perhaps. Brandeis was rather frenetic, though I understood that better after experiencing, some years later, the quiet sedateness of Princeton. The university had been established as the Jewish-sponsored, nonsectarian institution of higher education—the first in the nation—open to all. At its conception, Jewish students and teachers faced discrimination in many colleges and universities. Fortunately, the barriers to entry were beginning to fall in 1948. But there were other good reasons for this Jewish gift to American education. It called up an esprit among Jews that was often quite marvelous. It was especially receptive to the arts. I think Brandeis had an art museum before it had a science building. It brought a special perspective to the humanities and the social sciences. A people who had lost six million of their own in a holocaust looked upon the fate of humanity differently. Some initiatives didn't pan out, for instance, intercollegiate football. Benny Friedman, the former All-American quarterback at the University of Michigan, came to the campus to coach football. In theory, playing football would counter the supposed image of Jews as passive and supraintellectual. But Brandeis football descended to farce. Brandeis was as liberal and secular an institution as you could hope to find. There was no chaplain nor religious exercises of any kind. Yet the president and trustees erected not one, but three chapels—Protestant, Catholic, Jewish—in a striking architectural complex at a corner of the campus. To me it symbolized the nation's religious pluralism in complete accord with the First Amendment guarantees of religious freedom and separation of church and state. It strengthened all my sympathies in that direction.

Many students found in Lerner an inspiring teacher, and his course on American civilization was a huge success. He had an easygoing, mellifluous style, open to all and sundry, from which I might learn but could never hope to emulate. One of my colleagues, Frank Manuel, an erudite historian of ideas who taught the freshman course in Western civilization, was puzzled by this utterly unpedantic teacher with bushy black hair, dark pensive eyes, and the face of a roughened John Garfield.

> While many of us clung to the professorate as a secular priesthood, and pontificated from a formal elevated rostrum, suddenly in sauntered a breezy man who laughed easily and made others laugh, and sat on the edge of the platform—not up at the rostrum—dangling his feet, and conversed with an astonished body of students, as if he were in a market place—Socrates at play. . . . In a brazen act of democratization, he offered his class for criticism chapter after chapter of the manuscript of his great work on America as a civilization, instructing, debating, challenging the young men and women who were the most recent embodiment of this civilization. Before us pompous professors who were committed to education as a rehearsal of the past, [Lerner] flaunted the primacy of present things and the presence of future things.

Often, during his lecture, as Sandy Lakoff has reminded me, Lerner would turn in my direction and, looking for verification of some offhand comment on a historical matter, inquire of me, "Yes, Merrill?" Indeed, Lakoff says, the students' moniker for me was "Yes, Merrill."

During my first year full-time, I taught the year-long surveys in American history, American literature, and American constitutional law in addition to assisting in Lerner's big course. How I managed this feat, and the sheer audacity of it, now amazes me. But I was young, and that load of course preparation and teaching completed my apprenticeship in a career I yet little understood. Being new, absent all tradition, with no codes and none of the pathways laid out, with no very clear idea of what it should become, Brandeis was exhilarating one moment and aggravating the next. One liability for me, as I later realized, was that it prolonged my academic innocence. The professional ropes could not be learned there. It had no academic hierarchy, virtually no administration, no disciplinary demarcation of faculty, few colleagues, and no alumni except an invented "foster alumni." But it had a stimulating faculty withal, one in which Zionism and democratic socialism lived comfortably together. And it had a body of eager learners. The typical student hailed from Bayonne or Brooklyn or the Bronx, probably second generation of a Jewish family of modest means, and, although unpolished, endowed with a passion to learn and express oneself. When it came time for the first class to graduate in 1952, Brandeis held its collective breath as it waited to see how its students fared in the race for admission to the top graduate and professional schools. They, of course, passed the test with flying colors.

In 1951, as Brandeis grew, I was joined by a young colleague in American history, Leonard Levy, a freshly minted Ph.D. from Columbia University. His special field was constitutional history, and I was happy to surrender to him the course I had introduced. Leonard and I, with personalities 180 degrees apart, proved to be a good match. He gave himself unstintingly to the institution, while laying the foundation for a great scholarly career. Before long I surrendered the literature survey as well and was able to focus my teaching more closely in the field of American intellectual history. I kept my summers free for research to develop and extend my dissertation into a book, but my progress was slow. Fortunately, in 1955, a year after my wife and I had our first child, an opportunity came from Princeton for a three-year assistant professorship that allowed one year exclusively for research and writing. In 1958 I completed the manuscript of "The Jefferson Image in the American Mind" and delivered it to Oxford University Press with whom I had a contract for publication. With this Brandeis asked me to return, throwing an associate professorship with tenure into the bargain. I was pleased to accept.

The Jefferson Image in the American Mind appeared, at last, in 1960, and it met with unexpected success. Early in the new year it won the esteemed Bancroft Prize in American History. My fortieth year, 1961, was my annus mirabilis. In addition to receiving the Bancroft, which was awarded in a grand affair at Columbia University in

April, I was invited to address the American Philosophical Society in Philadelphia and also awarded a specially struck gold medal by the Thomas Jefferson Memorial Foundation at Monticello on the statesman-architect's birthday, April 13. Not long after, I was offered a contract by Oxford to write a substantial one-volume biography of Jefferson. In this connection, I was invited to apply for a Guggenheim Fellowship to commence that work. With the support of the two premier Jefferson scholars, Dumas Malone and Julian Boyd, the fellowship was awarded for the next academic year. This train of events culminated in 1962 when I was invited by the University of Virginia to succeed Malone as the Jefferson Foundation Professor of History. It was an offer not to be refused.

I have often reflected that my scholarly destiny, indeed my career, was fixed by the lucky choice of a doctoral dissertation topic. And that, in turn, might have been the result of my early reading of Vernon L. Parrington and, over many years, the *New Republic*. Certainly, that magazine more than anything else in my young life lighted the pathway to my intellectual maturity.

Acknowledgments

I am indebted to one old friend, William W. Abbot, for reading the first draft of my manuscript, and to a new friend, Nini Almy, for her reading and support virtually from beginning to end. To her the book is dedicated.

As always, I have to thank the Alderman Library, with its staff, of the University of Virginia. It boasts not one but two complete sets of the *New Republic* in hard copy, and it wholly met my research needs. Donna Packard furnished the word-processed manuscript, and Sara Davis, at the University of Missouri Press, was its engaged and skillful copyeditor.

I thank the following publishers for permission to quote passages from copyrighted works: from *W. H. Auden: Collected Poems,* edited by Edward Mendelson (copyright 1940, renewed 1968, by W. H. Auden) reprinted by permission of Random House, Inc.; from Langston Hughes, *Collected Poems,* edited by Arnold Rampersand (copyright 1994 by the Estate of Langston Hughes) reprinted by permission of Alfred A. Knopf, Inc., and by permission of Harold Ober Associates, Inc.

DATE DUE

Demco, Inc. 38-293